Internationales Jahrbuch Kommunikationsdesign | International Yearbook Communication Design   2004 | 2005

INTERNATIONALES JAHRBUCH KOMMUNIKATIONSDESIGN

Peter Zec (Hrsg. | Ed.)

INTERNATIONAL YEARBOOK COMMUNICATION DESIGN   2004|2005

avedition

INHALT

CONTENTS

Peter Zec

Prof. Dr. Peter Zec ist
geschäftsführender
Vorstand des Design
Zentrums Nordrhein
Westfalen und Pro-
fessor für Wirtschafts-
kommunikation an
der Fachhochschule
für Technik und Wirt-
schaft Berlin.

VORWORT DES HERAUSGEBERS

„Kommunikation ist riskant!" Mit dieser Erkenntnis steht der Soziologe Niklas Luhmann sicher nicht alleine da. Stets besteht das Risiko des Missverstehens oder sogar der Ablehnung. Der Aus-gang von Kommunikation ist prinzipiell ungewiss, da es immer ein anderer ist, der darüber ent-scheidet. Andererseits ist es aber gar nicht möglich, aus Angst vor dem Risiko vollkommen auf Kommunikation zu verzichten. Paul Watzlawick behauptet sogar ganz radikal: „Man kann nicht nicht kommunizieren!" Also gilt es, sich immer wieder von neuem dem Risiko der Kommunikation auszusetzen, jeweils verbunden mit der Hoffnung, dass es schon nicht zu schlimm ausgehen wird. Immerhin kommt es ja auch vor, dass Kommunikation zum gewünschten Erfolg führt.

Eine ganz besondere Art des Erfolgs mit Kommunikation wird in dem vorliegenden Jahrbuch doku-mentiert. Vorgestellt werden darin Arbeiten aus verschiedenen Bereichen des internationalen Kommunikationsdesigns, die von einer Experten-Jury im Rahmen des red dot award: communi-cation design 2004 als besonders gelungen ausgezeichnet worden sind. Angesichts der Vielzahl der Einreichungen (2.936 Arbeiten aus 27 Nationen) hatten die neun internationalen Juroren auch in diesem Jahr keine leichte Aufgabe. Hinzu kommt, dass das Niveau der eingereichten Arbeiten insgesamt als überdurchschnittlich hoch bewertet wurde. Ungeachtet dessen hat die Jury ihre stets hohen Qualitätsmaßstäbe aufrechterhalten und ein hartes wie auch faires Urteil gefällt.

Am Ende sind es weniger als acht Prozent aller Arbeiten, die mit einer Auszeichnung erfolgreich waren. Insgesamt wurde 198-mal das Qualitätssiegel „red dot" für herausragende Gestaltung verliehen. Darüber hinaus wurden weitere 31 Arbeiten als jeweils beste Leistungen in den zehn Wettbewerbskategorien mit der Auszeichnung „red dot: best of the best" gewürdigt.

Der mit 10.000 Euro dotierte Grand Prix geht in diesem Jahr erstmals in die USA. Ausgezeichnet wurde damit die Katalogreihe „CROP" von Segura Inc. aus Chicago. Neben dem Preisträger wur-den zwei weitere Arbeiten für den red dot: grand prix nominiert. Es handelt sich hierbei um die Anzeigenkampagne „Wörlitz – Ein Hort der Toleranz" von Heye & Partner in Unterhaching und um die Ausstellungsgestaltung „Wer's glaubt, wird selig?" von Jäger & Jäger aus Überlingen. Der mit 2.500 Euro dotierte Juniorpreis wird für den TV-Spot „Save your face!" an Daniel Janssen aus Hamburg verliehen. Nominiert waren hierfür ebenfalls die Internetseite www.slewe.nl von Niels Schrader aus Amsterdam sowie die Arbeit „Stadt- und Bürgerkommunikation – ein Corpo-rate-Identity-Konzept für die Stadt Wuppertal" von Nicolas Markwald und Nina Neusitzer aus Wuppertal.

PREFACE BY THE EDITOR

Peter Zec

Prof. Dr. Peter Zec
is President of the
Design Zentrum
Nordrhein Westfalen
in Essen, and pro-
fessor of business
communication at
the Fachhochschule
für Technik und Wirt-
schaft in Berlin.

"Communication is risky!" Niklas Luhmann, the sociologist, is by no means the only one to have realized this. The risk of being misunderstood, or even of being rejected, is a constant fact of life. It is in the very nature of communication that its outcome is uncertain because it is always some-one else who decides what this outcome is. On the other hand, it is just not possible to stop communicating for fear of this. Paul Watzlawick makes a more radical claim: "You cannot not communicate!" One is forced to repeatedly confront the risk of communication, each time in the hope that the results won't be too bad. After all, it has been known that communication some-times does lead to the desired success.

A very special example of the success of communication is documented in this yearbook. It presents work from various areas of international communication design, all of which have been selected for acclaim by a jury of experts for the "red dot award: communication design 2004". Once again this year, the nine international jurors had their work cut out for them with 2,936 submissions being made from 27 countries. This task was not made easier as the quality of the submissions was overall higher than normal. In spite of this, the jury has maintained its high quality standards and made a hard but fair choice for this year's award. In the end, less than 8 % of all work submitted managed to win an award. Overall, the red dot was awarded 198 times for excellent design. In addition, a further 31 works were selected for the "red dot: best of the best" award for the best work in each of the ten categories of the competition.

For the first time, the grand prix of 10,000 euro goes to the USA in recognition of the catalogue series "CROP" from Segura Inc., Chicago. In addition to the main prize winner, two other works were nominated for the "red dot: grand prix". These were the advertising campaign under the title "Wörlitz – Ein Hort der Toleranz" from Heye & Partner in Unterhaching and the exhibition stand design, "Wer's glaubt, wird selig?" from Jäger & Jäger in Überlingen.

The Junior Prize of 2,500 euro was awarded to Daniel Janssen from Hamburg for his TV com-mercial "save your face". The internet site www.slewe.nl by Niels Schrader from Amsterdam was also nominated here as was the work "Stadt- und Bürgerkommunikation – ein Corporate-Identity-Konzept für die Stadt Wuppertal" from Nicolas Markwald and Nina Neusitzer from Wuppertal.

This year was also the first time the "red dot: digital media" was awarded. This prize goes to the best work submitted by entrants of the digital media category of the competition. The

Erstmalig in diesem Jahr wurde der Sonderpreis „red dot: digital media" ausgelobt. Er wird an die beste Arbeit unter allen Wettbewerbsteilnehmern im Bereich der digitalen Medien vergeben. Ausgezeichnet wurde die interaktive Installation „floating.numbers", die das Designstudio Art+Com für eine Sonderausstellung des Jüdischen Museums in Berlin realisiert hat.

Durch die Aufrechterhaltung der hohen Qualitätsmaßstäbe und anspruchsvollen Bewertungskriterien sorgen die Juroren Jahr für Jahr dafür, dass der red dot award: communication design weltweit zu den anspruchsvollsten und zugleich begehrtesten Wettbewerben zählt. Die Jury wählt nur wenige Arbeiten aus. Umso mehr ist dabei der Erfolg einer Auszeichnung von ganz besonderem Wert, auf die man zu Recht sehr stolz sein darf.

Kommunikation kann in vielen verschiedenen Formen geschehen. Sie kann betont sachlich sein und sich auf rationale Argumente gründen. Genauso ist es möglich, sehr stark an Gefühle und die sinnliche Wahrnehmung in der Kommunikation zu appellieren. Auffällig ist in diesem Jahr, dass in der Unternehmenskommunikation die rein sachliche Information nur noch selten für sich allein steht. Vielmehr wird diese zunehmend in ein Gefüge aus Zusatzinformationen eingebettet, das aus sinnlich ansprechenden Visualisierungen und anspruchsvoller Gestaltung besteht: die Adressaten werden auf diese Weise verstärkt auf einer Gefühlsebene angesprochen. So ist man bestrebt, sympathisch und freundlich aufgeschlossen zu wirken, um potentielle Kunden oder aber auch Geschäftsfreunde und Mitarbeiter an das Unternehmen zu binden. Dies gilt ebenfalls, wenn man Menschen für eine Marke oder die Teilnahme an einem Ereignis gewinnen möchte.

Besonders deutlich zeigt sich diese Tendenz der emotional verstärkten Ansprache im Bereich der Finanz- und Unternehmenskommunikation. So versuchen zahlreiche Unternehmen in ihren Geschäftsberichten nicht mehr nur mit Fakten und Zahlen zu beeindrucken, sondern betreiben einen großen Aufwand an sinnlicher Darstellung und Inszenierung, um durch eine gesteigerte emotionale Ansprachequalität das Vertrauen von Anlegern, Investoren und Kunden zu gewinnen oder wieder zu erlangen. Dies gilt insbesondere für börsennotierte Unternehmen, die anscheinend erkannt haben, dass sie verstärkt auf die Qualitäten eines anspruchsvollen und emotional fesselnden Kommunikationsdesigns setzen müssen. Für Agenturen und Designer entsteht dadurch die Herausforderung, bei der Gestaltung von Geschäftsberichten die erforderliche Sachlichkeit der Fakten und Zahlen mit einer emotionalen und zugleich einprägsamen Form der ästhetischen

opening prize was awarded to the interactive installation "floating.numbers" from design studio Art+Com for a special exhibition staged by the Jewish Museum in Berlin.

By constantly insisting on high quality standards and sticking to rigorous judging criteria, the jurors ensure that the "red dot award: communication design" remains, year for year, one of the toughest and thus most prestigious competitions worldwide. The jury only selects a few works for acclaim. This only increases the aura of winning an award, something about which the prize-winners can be deservedly proud.

Communication can take many forms. It can be consciously objective and based on rational arguments. But it can just as easily make a strong appeal to the emotions and sensibilities of the audience. A noticeable factor this year was that, in corporate communication, purely objective information very rarely stood alone. Rather, it is nowadays more common to embed objective facts and figures in a matrix of additional information composed of aesthetic visualizations and quality design. In this way, an attempt is made to appeal and appear open to contact in order to bind potential customers or even business associates and employees to the enterprise, or to win them for a brand or encourage them to participate in an event.

This trend was especially apparent in the emotionally reinforced messages being made in the sector of financial and corporate communication. The annual reports of a large number of companies no longer try to impress their audience with a mere presentation of the facts and figures but now go to great efforts to present themselves in a manner that is both aesthetic and tries to make the right associations so as to win – or win back – the confidence of share-holders, investors and customers by raising the emotional content of their address. This espe-cially applies to publicly listed companies who have apparently realized that they must increas-ingly rely on the qualities of exceptional communication design which is also emotionally appealing. For agencies and designers this translates into a design challenge: simultaneously respecting the objectivity by which facts and figures should be presented in an annual report but nevertheless presenting these in an aesthetic form of communication that appeals to the emotions and makes a lasting impression. The best results in this area have been presented in this yearbook.

When it came to corporate internet sites the jurors observed two contrary trends. Whether a company should even have an internet site is no longer an issue. The debate today has shifted

Kommunikation in Einklang zu bringen. Die besten Ergebnisse auf diesem Gebiet werden in dem vorliegenden Jahrbuch vorgestellt.

Im Bereich der Internetauftritte von Unternehmen beobachteten die Juroren zwei gegenläufige Entwicklungen. Dabei steht heute nicht mehr die Frage im Vordergrund, ob Firmen überhaupt eine Online-Präsenz haben, sondern eher, wie intensiv sie dieses Medium nutzen. Ein Teil der Internetauftritte hält zunehmend wohl geordnete Informationen mit einer erstaunlichen Übersichtlichkeit bereit und wird so mehr und mehr zu einem öffentlichen Archiv des Betreibers. Der Informationsgehalt dieser Seiten geht in der Regel weit über das Notwendige hinaus und bietet einen echten Mehrwert. Die andere Gruppe zielt darauf ab, den Nutzer mittels halb spielerischer, halb informativer Aktivitäten möglichst lange auf der eigenen Website zu halten. Spiele im Internet etwa werden so zu einem verlängerten Arm der Unternehmenskommunikation.

Deutlich wird in diesem Bereich auch, dass bei Internetauftritten mit einer klar bestimmbaren Gruppe von Adressaten der Gestaltungsspielraum für Kommunikationsdesigner wesentlich größer ist als bei Seiten, die sich an ein mehr oder weniger anonymes Massenpublikum wenden. Massenkommunikation verdirbt die Qualität. Bei einer gezielten Teilansprache kennt man seine Klientel und kann deren Bedürfnissen nicht nur inhaltlich, sondern auch durch eine entsprechende Gestaltung besser gerecht werden.

Eine andere Tendenz, die sich bereits während der letzten Wettbewerbe langsam herauskristallisiert hat, ist die abnehmende Bedeutung des Plakates als verbreitete Kommunikationsform. Das war im red dot award: communication design 2004 sowohl quantitativ als auch qualitativ nicht mehr zu übersehen. Dies ist nicht zuletzt darauf zurückzuführen, dass die audiovisuellen Medien dem Plakat als Kommunikationsform den Rang ablaufen. Das Plakat steckt in der Krise. Insbesondere im Kulturbereich finden sich nur noch wenige anspruchsvolle Plakate. Hier ist die Finanznot der öffentlichen Haushalte deutlich zu spüren. Allein in den osteuropäischen Ländern ist die Plakatkunst noch stark verbreitet. Niemand vermag jedoch vorauszusehen, ob die Krise des Plakates von Dauer ist und damit ein grundlegender Wandel dieser Kommunikationsform eintreten wird oder ob es sich nur um ein temporäres Phänomen der Sparsamkeit seitens der Auftraggeber handelt. Die Zukunft wird es uns zeigen.

An der Durchführung des diesjährigen Wettbewerbs haben wieder einmal zahlreiche Freunde, Partner, Mitarbeiter und Förderer mitgewirkt, ohne deren Engagement weder das vorliegende

to how extensively a company should be using this medium. Some of the internet sites provide increasingly better organized information with an amazing clarity and are thus evolving to become a public archive of the operator. Generally, the amount of information on these sites goes well beyond what is required and offers real added value. The other group aims at keeping the users on the website as long as possible by offering half-playful, half-informative activities. In this way, even internet games are becoming another branch of corporate communication.

It has also become clear that there are many more design possibilities available to communication designers of internet sites that target a clearly identified audience than there are for sites which address a more or less anonymous mass audience. Mass communication ruins the quality. In a targeted address, one knows one's clientele and can better satisfy their needs both in terms of content and by generating a design equal to the task.

Another development, which was already slowly crystallizing over the course of recent competitions, is that the poster as a means of mass communication is losing significance. This trend could no longer be overlooked during the "red dot award: communication design 2004" where both the numbers and the quality of entries had fallen. One not insignificant factor in this trend is that, as a form of communication, audiovisual media have come to overshadow the poster. Poster design is in a crisis. There are only a handful of excellent posters to be seen, particularly in the cultural sphere. This is a clear indication of the financial straits that public bodies currently find themselves in. Posters are now only widespread in Eastern European countries. However, nobody can say whether this crisis is a lasting one leading to a fundamental change in this form of communication or whether this is only a temporary phenomenon caused by the frugality of the client group. We will know better in future.

Once again, countless friends, partners, employees and promoters have contributed to the success of this year's competition. Without their commitment and enthusiasm this yearbook and the event itself would hardly have been possible. I would like to thank all concerned.

Special thanks go to the largest insurance agency of Allianz, Krenzler Graf Biermann OHG from Essen, who donated the prize money for the "red dot: grand prix". My thanks also go to the AGD Alliance of German Designers for contributing the prize money for the "red dot: junior prize". I would also like to express my gratitude to all official partners of the competition: AGI (Alliance Graphique Internationale), BDG (Bund Deutscher Grafik-Designer), BNO (Beroepsorganisatie

Jahrbuch noch die Veranstaltung insgesamt möglich gewesen wäre. Hierfür möchte ich mich bei allen Beteiligten bedanken.

Besonderer Dank gebührt der größten deutschen Generalvertretung der Allianz, Krenzler Graf Biermann OHG aus Essen, die das Preisgeld des red dot: grand prix gestiftet hat. Ferner gilt mein Dank der AGD Alliance of German Designers für die Stiftung des Preisgeldes des red dot: junior prize.

Mein Dank gilt auch allen offiziellen Partnern des Wettbewerbs: AGI (Alliance Graphique Internationale), BDG (Bund Deutscher Grafik-Designer), BNO (Beroepsorganisatie Nederlandse Ontwerpers), dmmv (Deutscher Multimedia Verband), Page (Designzeitschrift), SGD (Swiss Graphic Designers) und VGD (Verband der Grafik-Designer).

Ein besonderer Dank gebührt allen Juroren des Wettbewerbs für die engagierte Zusammenarbeit. Und last but not least möchte ich allen teilnehmenden Designern, Agenturen und Unternehmern herzlich für ihren Mut und ihre Lust danken, ihre Arbeiten zur Diskussion zu stellen. Erst dadurch machen Sie den Wettbewerb Jahr für Jahr möglich!

Nederlandse Ontwerpers), dmmv (Deutscher Multimedia Verband), Page (Designzeitschrift), SGD (Swiss Graphic Designers) and VGD (Verband der Grafik-Designer).
Likewise, I am very grateful for the energy and efforts of all jurors of the competition. Last but not least, I would like to say thanks to all the designers, agencies and companies who have taken part in this year's competition, for their courage and their willingness to put their work up for discussion. It is you who make the competition possible, year after year!

Rainer Zimmermann

Dr. Rainer Zimmermann, Herausgeber des „Handbuchs der Unternehmenskommunikation", ist seit 1995 Agenturchef von KohtesKlewes, seit 1999 geschäftsführender Gesellschafter und Chief Executive Officer der BBDO Germany, seit 2004 Director BBDO Europe sowie CEO Pleon und europaweit für das Geschäftsfeld Public Relations verantwortlich.

TRUESIGN

Anstelle fremder Denkofferten den eigenen Gegenstand denken

Wörter zerfallen im Mund wie modrige Pilze. Sie schmecken nicht mehr nach Bedeutung. Deckenhänger sind Kommunikation, Klingeltöne sind Kommunikation, ein Gespräch mit meiner Frau ist es auch. Schröder trägt einen Brioni-Anzug. Das ist symbolische Kommunikation. Bela Anda erklärt die Agenda 2010. Das ist politische Kommunikation. Ackermann erhebt seine Hand zum Victory-Zeichen, das ist entgleiste Kommunikation. Meine Werbeagentur heißt jetzt Kommunikationsagentur, meine PR-Agentur übrigens auch. Alles ist Kommunikation. Die Welt quillt über von Kommunikationsexperten, sie verlegen Glasfaserkabel, koordinieren Satelliten, reparieren Telefonanlagen, schreiben Reden für den Vorstandsvorsitzenden, betreiben Change Management oder arrangieren die Petits Fours bei einem Event, natürlich streng nach den CD-Richtlinien. Kommunikation kann alles, Kommunikation muss alles. Die Welt spricht nun einmal, überall lauern Botschaften.

Die Sprache der Dinge, da sind wir beim Design. Landschaftsarchitektur ist jetzt Ambient Design, mein Gärtner weiß es noch nicht. Hairdesign, Gel muss sein, Sounddesign, das klingt so fein. Aber wie gesagt, die Sprache der Dinge muss in die Sprache der Menschen überführt werden. Deshalb gibt es jetzt Kommunikationsdesign. Das ist natürlich dialektisch zu sehen. Kommunikationsdesigner designen Kommunikation und kommunizieren Design. Die berühmteste Kommunikationsdesignerin Deutschlands ist ohne Zweifel Heidi Klum. Sie designt für Birkenstock, sie kommuniziert ständig, verbal und vor allem nonverbal, beides zusammen auch medial. Heidi, das spürt man, betreibt natürlich auch strategisches Kommunikationsdesign im Hinblick auf ihre eigene Vermarktung. Sie ist ja ihr eigenes Produkt. Das nennt man dann Selfdesign. Dieser neue Trend ersetzt die alte, authentizitätshungrige Selbstverwirklichung, beginnt bei Functional Food, Tattoos, Piercings und endet bei der plastischen Chirurgie und genetischem Design. Bis in die letzten Winkel dieses Planeten ist Design schon vorgedrungen, jetzt wendet der Mensch es auf sich selbst an. So formbar wie die Welt ist nun auch die eigene Individualität. Weil sie immer weicher, haltloser wird. Formbar eben. Designbedürftig. Kann Design für Designbedürftige noch gutes Design sein?

Wahrscheinlich war es nötig, die ungepflegte Brücke zwischen Kommunikation und Design in einem Begriff zu versöhnen. Marktpolitisch ist „Kommunikationsdesign" eine gute Idee. Im Sinne einer Abgrenzung des Produktdesigns von anderen Anwendungsfeldern des Designs befördert

TRUESIGN

Rainer Zimmermann

Original design concepts are called for not a mere rehashing of borrowed ideas
Words crumble in the mouth like rotting mushrooms. They lose their taste. And they lose their meaning. POS danglers are communication, ringing tones are communication, so is a talk with my wife. Chancellor Schröder wears a suit from Brioni. That is symbolic communication. Bela Anda proclaims the Agenda 2010. That is political communication. Ackermann raises his hand in a sign of victory. Here, communication has gone off the rails. My advertising agency is now called a communication agency. My PR agency is too. Everything is communication. The world is brimming with communication experts. They are laying fiber optic cable, coordinating satellites, repairing telephone systems, writing speeches for CEOs, implementing change management or arranging the petit fours for an event – in strict accordance with CD guidelines goes without saying. Communication can do everything. Communication must do everything. The world is speaking – messages are on the prowl everywhere.

The language of objects – this brings us to design. Landscape architecture is now called ambient design, but my gardener doesn't know it yet. Hair design, has to be gel, acoustic design, rings like a bell. But, as we all know, the language of objects has to be translated into a language understood by people. So now we have communication design. Of course, this should be understood dialectically. Communication designers design communication and communicate design. Without a doubt, Heidi Klum is Germany's most famous communication designer. She designs for Birkenstock, communicates constantly, both verbally and, more importantly, non-verbally, but most importantly of all, on all media. You can feel it: Heidi is pursuing strategic communication design to market herself. She is her own product. This is self-design, a new trend which is replacing the old concept of self-realization with its hungering for authenticity. It starts with functional food, tattoos and piercing and ends with plastic surgery and genetic modification. Design has reached the farthest corners of the Earth and humankind is now applying it to itself. The world can be manipulated, but so too can one's own individuality – because it is losing its focus, and losing its roots in the process. Becoming malleable in fact. In need of design.
Can design for those in need of design still be good design?
Probably the rusty old bridge between communication and design had to be renewed sooner or later with a new term. For marketing strategy, "communication design" is a good idea. However, in terms of distinguishing product design from other design fields, the term already manifests

Dr. Rainer Zimmermann, Publisher of "Das Handbuch der Unternehmenskommunikation" (Manual of Corporate Communication) has been Office Manager of KohtesKlewes since 1995, Managing Director and CEO of BBDO Germany since 1999, and Director of BBDO Europe since 2004 as well as CEO of Pleon where he is responsible for Public Relations in Europe.

der Begriff allerdings schon die anschwellende Unverbindlichkeit und Virtualisierung von Design. Die Frage ist also, ob K-Design nicht vom Wesentlichen und Eigentlichen wegführt. Die Frage ist, ob fremde Wissenschaftsofferten, fremde Denkmodelle das ureigene Denken des Designs nicht innerlich aushöhlen. Eine Philosophie, die psychologisiert, verliert ihren Gegenstand aus dem Auge. Design, das auf Kommunikation schielt, sieht nicht mehr klar genug. „Um Himmels willen keinen Designer", schrie neulich ein gebildeter CEO anlässlich der Umgestaltung seines Headquarters, „bringen Sie mir einen echten Architekten, von mir aus auch einen Schreiner." Kurz darauf bin ich zugegen, als ein Brand Manager bei der Layoutpräsentation seines internationalen Kundenmagazins ausrastet: „Ich will nicht cross, ich will nicht fusion, ich will nicht von allem etwas und nichts so richtig, ich will die reine Substanz. Hört endlich auf, mir diese multikulturelle, interdisziplinäre Designsuppe zu servieren". Konvergenz ist eben das Gegenteil von Position. Man kann auch von Verwässerung sprechen.

Um Positionen aber geht es. Um eigenständige Positionen. Wer sein Heil in Fusionen sucht, hat offensichtlich eine schwache Position, die er anreichern möchte mit fremden, das heißt: nicht eigenen Bedeutungen. Design hat die Fusion mit Kommunikation nicht nötig. Sie schadet sogar. Ich höre mich schon rufen: „Ich will keinen Kommunikationsdesigner, bringen Sie mir einen richtigen Designer, so wie früher". Der red dot design award zeichnet vorbildliches Design aus. Design, das diesen Namen verdient. Truesign, sollte man vielleicht sagen. Es kann doch nicht sein, dass Design bloß ein anderes Wort für Gestaltung ist. Ich dachte eigentlich immer, dass wahres Design erst da anfängt, wo Gestaltung aufhört. Ich dachte immer, Design hätte mehr mit Demut als mit Hochmut zu tun. Falls das stimmt, sollten Designer sich darauf konzentrieren, den eigenen Gegenstand zu denken anstatt irgendwo im Niemandsland zwischen Big Brand Ideas, Kommunikationsmanagement und Marketingprozessen herumzugestalten. Ich denke, nur ein solches Design, das nicht auf Kommunikation achtet, kann Kommunikation letztlich noch prägen. Wie sagte doch Jerry Garcia, einer der Gründer von Grateful Dead: „We never wanted to make music that was better or different. We always wanted to make music that only we could do".

the looming vagueness and virtualization inherent in design. So the real issue is whether communication design is not actually leading us away from significance and reality. The question is whether the offerings made by other people's philosophies, other people's thought structures, are not actually hollowing out one's own original design concept. A philosophy which psychologizes its subject matter loses sight of its object. Design that steals a glance at communication, is no longer focusing on the way ahead. "For heaven's sake, no designers!" cried a rather sophisticated CEO recently when it came to redesigning the company's headquarters, "bring me a genuine architect – as far as I'm concerned, it can be a joiner." Shortly afterwards I was present when a brand manager lost his cool during the presentation of a new layout: "I don't want cross, I don't want fusion, I don't want a bit of everything and nothing done right, I want substance, pure substance. Stop serving up this multi-cultural, interdisciplinary designer stew." He is right: convergence is the antithesis of having a clear position. You could also call it dilution.
But having a position is what it is all about. An independent position. Whoever looks to fusion for his salvation obviously has a weak position that he needs to enrich with foreign input, i.e. meanings that are not his own. Design does not need any fusion with communication. It would even be harmful. I can already hear myself saying, "I don't want a communication designer, bring me a genuine designer, like in the old days." The Red Dot Award is for exemplary design. Design that deserves the name. Truesign, is perhaps the right term for it. True design has to be more than the mere act of designing. I always thought that true design starts where mere designing stops. I always thought that true design had more to do with humility than with arrogance. If I am right, the designer should concentrate on the conception of his or her own design object rather than fiddling around in the no man's land between big brand ideas, communication management and marketing processes. I sincerely believe that only design which does not concentrate on communication can, in the end, actually have a real impact on communication. As Jerry Garcia of the Grateful Dead put it, "We never wanted to make music that was better or different. We always wanted to make music that only we could do".

RED DOT GRAND PRIX

RED DOT: GRAND PRIX

Zum ersten Mal geht die höchste Ehrenauszeichnung, der red dot: grand prix, in diesem Jahr in die USA. Ausgezeichnet wurde die Katalogreihe „CROP" von Segura Inc. in Chicago. Das Preisgeld in Höhe von 10.000 Euro wird von Krenzler Graf Biermann OHG, Allianz Group in Essen gestiftet. Ebenfalls für den Grand Prix nominiert waren die Werbekampagne „Wörlitz – Ein Hort der Toleranz" von Heye & Partner in Unterhaching und das Ausstellungsdesign „Wer's glaubt, wird selig?" von Jäger & Jäger in Überlingen.

„CROP" ist eine großformatige Katalogserie für Corbis Stock Photography – im Rahmen eines Rebranding wurden bisher sieben Stück produziert. Seit fast zwei Jahren betreut Segura Inc. den Kunden. Die Kataloge werden kostenlos abgegeben und erscheinen in einer Auflage von 30.000 Stück. Bei der Herstellung kommen außergewöhnlich viele verschiedene Papiere und Drucktechniken zum Einsatz, der Inhalt ist jedes Mal anders, die Verpackung wird extra angefertigt. Gründer und Inhaber des Designbüros Segura Inc. ist Carlos Segura; er ist gleichzeitig Creative Director der „CROP"-Kataloge. Nachdem er über zehn Jahre für bedeutende Agenturen wie HCM Marsteller, Young & Rubicam, DDB Needham und BBDO in Pittsburgh und Chicago gearbeitet hatte, gründete er 1991 eine eigene Firma, um einen kreativeren Zugang zum Design verwirklichen zu können. Der unmittelbare Erfolg der Segura Inc. veranlasste ihn 1994, die [T-26] Digital Type Foundry zu gründen, die heute führend im unabhängigen Fontdesign ist. Weitere Informationen unter www.segura-inc.com.

RED DOT: GRAND PRIX

This is the first year that the supreme distinction of the "red dot: grand prix" has gone to the USA, being awarded to the "CROP" catalogue series from Segura Inc., Chicago. The prize of 10,000 euro is endowed by the company Krenzler Graf Biermann OHG, Allianz Group from Essen. Also nominated for the grand prix were the advertising campaign titled "Wörlitz – Ein Hort der Toleranz" from Heye & Partner in Unterhaching and the exhibition stand design titled "Wer's glaubt, wird selig?" from Jäger & Jäger in Überlingen.

"CROP" is a large format product catalogue series for the client Corbis Stock Photography. There have been seven produced to date as part of a re-branding effort. Segura Inc. have been involved with the client for almost two years. While the catalogues are free, print runs are limited to 30,000 and include an extraordinary number of different papers, printing techniques and varied content, all in specially produced packaging.

Founder and principal of the design company Segura Inc. is Carlos Segura, who is also the creative director of the "CROP" catalogues. After working for more than a decade in several prominent agencies such as HCM Marsteller, Young & Rubicam, DDB Needham or BBDO, both in Pittsburgh and Chicago, he decided to pursue a more creative approach to design by founding his own firm in 1991. With the instant success of Segura Inc., he founded [T-26] Digital Type Foundry in 1994, which is one of today's leading promoters of independent font design. For more information visit www.segura-inc.com.

LUCY LIU

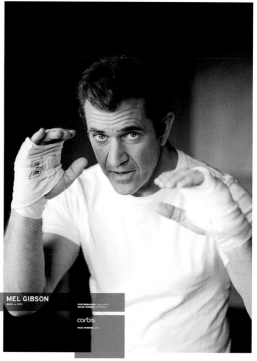

MEL GIBSON

Winner of the
red dot: grand prix

TITLE
"Crop" Series

TYPE OF WORK
Large-format
catalogues

CLIENT
Corbis, Seattle

APPEARED IN
2004

DESIGN
Segura Inc., Chicago
Creative direction:
Carlos Segura
Design:
Carlos Segura,
Dave Weik, Tnop,
Chris May, Ryan
Halvorsen

Wörlitz und die Toleranz
Es war einmal ein Land, da war die
Regierung die höchste moralische Instanz.

War dies das gelobte Land? Über Jahrhunderte
waren die Juden in ganz Europa Vertreibungen
und Verfolgungen ausgesetzt. Man grenzte
sie aus, man sperrte sie in Gettos. Immer
waren sie Bürger zweiter Klasse, denen man
nur die wenigen Berufe zugestand, die
Christen nicht ausüben durften - z.B. Geld-
verleih. (An Geldgeschäften zu verdienen
galt damals noch als unchristlich.) Und dann
erhob sich plötzlich diese Insel der Güte aus dem Meer des Schlechten. Nur ein kleines
Provinzfürstentum, aber regiert von einem Menschenfreund.

Fürst Leopold III. Friedrich Franz von Anhalt-Dessau (1740-1817) hatte sein Miniaturländchen
aus armseligen Anfängen in einen florierenden Musterstaat verwandelt, in dem man die Aufklärung
nicht nur predigte, sondern auch praktizierte. Juden waren ohne Vorbehalte willkommen. Sie
durften sich sogar als Bauern und Handwerker niederlassen, was in anderen deutschen Ländern
völlig undenkbar war. Jüdische Schulen wurden gegründet und sogar die erste jüdische Zeitung
in Deutschland. Der Philosoph Moses Mendelssohn, den Lessing als Vorbild für sein Drama
"Nathan der Weise" wählte, gehörte wie Goethe, Klopstock und Wieland zum Gelehrtenkreis, den
der Fürst um sich scharte.

Als die jüdische Gemeinde einen Gebetsraum suchte, schenkte Fürst Franz ihr einen Tempel
in seinem Wörlitzer Garten, der so zum einzigen Schloßpark in Deutschland wurde, in dem eine
Synagoge steht. Übrigens gleich neben der protestantischen Kirche, als sichtbares Zeichen
religiöser Gleichberechtigung. Wer will, kann all dies heute noch bestaunen. Das Wörlitzer
Gartenreich von Franz dem Friedfertigen hat alle Kriege und Ideologien überdauert und wurde vor
kurzem in den erlauchten Kreis des UNESCO-Weltkulturerbes aufgenommen. Mit einem Spaziergang
durch die weitläufigen Anlagen tauchen Sie in eine der schönsten Epochen deutscher Geschichte
ein und genießen zugleich ein überwältigendes Landschaftserlebnis. Denn die Saat der Aufklärung
ist aufgegangen und steht nun in voller Kraft und Blüte. Wenigstens hier.
Wörlitz. Ein Hort der Toleranz.

Das Gartenreich Dessau Wörlitz und seine Freunde bedanken sich bei der Deutschen Bank AG und bei der ZEIT, die das Erscheinen dieser Anzeige ermöglicht haben.

Nominated for the
red dot: grand prix

TITLE
Wörlitz. Ein Hort der
Toleranz.

TYPE OF WORK
Advertisements in
daily newspapers

CLIENT
Kulturstiftung
DessauWörlitz,
Dessau

APPEARED IN
11|2003

DESIGN
Heye & Partner GmbH,
Unterhaching
Ralph Taubenberger,
Karl Armer,
Beate Gronemann,
Monika Raber,
René Wentzel,
Lutz Winkler

Nominated for the
red dot: grand prix

TITLE
Wer's glaubt,
wird selig?

TYPE OF WORK
Exhibition design

CLIENT
Zisterzienserstift
Zwettl, Zwettl

APPEARED IN
05|2002

DESIGN
Jäger & Jäger,
Überlingen

RED DOT JUNIOR PRIZE

RED DOT: JUNIOR PRIZE

In diesem Jahr geht der red dot: junior prize für die beste und originellste studentische Arbeit aus den Bereichen Foto-, Grafik- und Kommunikationsdesign an Daniel Janssen aus Hamburg für seinen TV-Spot „Save your face!". Die AGD Alliance of German Designers stiftete zum fünften Mal den mit 2.500 Euro dotierten Preis. Nominiert waren hierfür ebenfalls die Internetseite www.slewe.nl von Niels Schrader aus Amsterdam sowie die Arbeit „Stadt- und Bürgerkommunikation – ein Corporate-Identity-Konzept für die Stadt Wuppertal" von Nicolas Markwald und Nina Neusitzer aus Wuppertal.

Der Film „Save your face!" ist ein fiktiver Social Spot für Amnesty International. Brutale Kriegsszenen reihen sich aneinander. Ein Soldat wird für seine „Verdienste" mit Orden ausgezeichnet. Mit jedem Orden schwindet ein Stück von ihm. Er verliert sein Gesicht. Die raue Kriegs-Szenerie wird durch Sprühschablonen-Ästhetik unterstützt. Der verzerrte Background-Song „Amazing Grace" betont die bedrückende Atmosphäre.

Die Jury zeigte sich tief beeindruckt: „Dem Gewinner des red dot: junior prize gilt unsere uneingeschränkte Anerkennung für diese eindrucksvolle Arbeit. Der Film ließ den Atem stocken in seiner präzisen, dramaturgischen und klaren Aussage. Deutlicher kann man die Sinnlosigkeit eines Krieges kaum darstellen."

Daniel Janssen, geboren 1973, arbeitete als Graveurmeister in Düsseldorf und studiert seit 2000 Kommunikationsdesign an der Hochschule für Angewandte Wissenschaften Hamburg. Der Film ist eine Semesterarbeit. Neben dem Studium arbeitet Janssen in den Bereichen Print Design, Type Design und Screen Design im eigenen Büro für Gestaltung: www.bfgjanssen.de.

RED DOT: JUNIOR PRIZE

This year the "red dot: junior prize" for the best and most original undergraduate work in the field of photography, graphic design and communication design goes to Daniel Janssen from Hamburg for his TV commercial, "Save your face!" For the fifth time now, the AGD Alliance of German Designers has donated the prize money of 2,500 euros. The internet site, www.slewe.nl from Niels Schrader in Amsterdam was also nominated here as was the work "Stadt- und Bürger-kommunikation – ein Corporate-Identity-Konzept für die Stadt Wuppertal" from Nicolas Mark-wald and Nina Neusitzer from Wuppertal.

The film "Save your face!" is a fictitious commercial with social content for Amnesty International. Brutal war scenes are displayed in sequence. A soldier is decorated with medals for his "merits". With each medal, a piece of him disappears until he loses his face. The violent war scenes are enhanced by the effect of air-brushed stencils. The distorted background song, "Amazing Grace" only adds to the oppressive atmosphere.

The jury was very impressed: "The winner of the 'red dot: junior prize' has won our unbounded recognition for this amazing work. The precise, dramaturgical and unambiguous statement of the film leaves you breathless. The senselessness of war cannot be presented in a clearer way." Daniel Janssen, born in 1973, worked as a professional engraver in Düsseldorf and has been studying communication design at the Hochschule für Angewandte Wissenschaften (University of Applied Sciences) in Hamburg since 2000. The film is his studio work for one semester. In addition to his studies, Janssen is working in the fields of print design, type design, and screen design at his own design office: www.bfgjanssen.de.

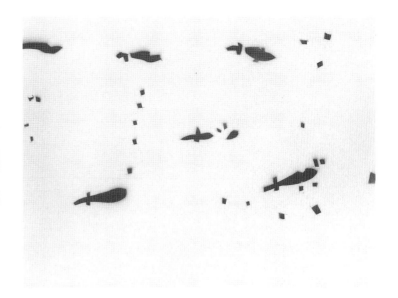

Winner of the
red dot: junior prize

TITLE
Save your face!

TYPE OF WORK
TV spot, studio work
for one semester

APPEARED IN
09|2003

DESIGN
Daniel Janssen,
Hamburg

Nominated for the
red dot: junior prize

TITLE
www.slewe.nl

TYPE OF WORK
Website

CLIENT
Martita Slewe
Slewe Gallery,
Amsterdam
Irma Boom Office,
Amsterdam

APPEARED IN
04|2004

DESIGN
Niels Schrader,
Amsterdam

SLEWE GALERII | MARTITA SLEWI | OPEN ON | MEMBER OF TH
KERKSTRAAT 1 | T: +31 20 625 7 | TUESDAY TO SA | N.G.A. – NETHER
1017 GD AMSTI | F: +31 20 421 4 | FROM 1 TO 6 P. | GALLERY ASSO

ARTISTS OF THE GALLERY: STEVEN AALDERS,
MERINA BEEKMAN, FRANK VAN DEN BROECK,
ADAM COLTON, IAN DAVENPORT, PETER DAVIS,
PAUL DRISSEN, MARTIN GERWERS,
JORIS GEURTS, ROBBERT-JAN GIJZEN,
CALLUM INNES, MICHAEL JACKLIN, ZEBEDEE JONES,
MARTINA KLEIN, KRIJN DE KONING, INGO MELLER

PREVIOUS EXHII | CURRENT EXHI | NEXT EXHIBITIC | ART FAIRS
| 10 YEARS SLEW | KRIJN DE KONII |
COLOPHON. | BOOKS | TO READ THE EN | REFRESH COLOU
UPDATE: OCTOE | | TEXTS, PLEASE I |

STEVEN AALD | | SOLO I | | GROUI
*1959, MIDD | 2004 | SLEWE | 2004 | MOND
LIVES AND W | 2002 | 'VERTI | 2003 | 'UP TO
| | GENT (| | MUSE
BACK TO IND | 2001 | SLEWE | | 'BECON
| | CCNOA | | OF HY
| 1998 | SLEWE | 2002 | STADS
| 1995 | SLEWE | | 'AMON
| 1993 | REUTE | | STEDE
| 1992 | REUTE | 1999 | SLEWI
| 1988 | JURKA | | 'RECEN
| | CASA | | STEDE
| 1987 | JURKA | 1998 | 'THE CI
| | | | GMURI

Stadt Wuppertal

Abstammungsurkunde

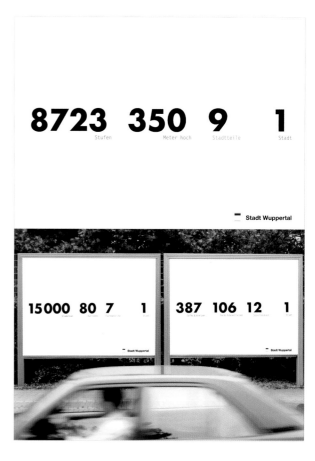

8723 350 9 1
Stufen Meter hoch Stadtteile Stadt

Stadt Wuppertal

15000 80 7 1   387 106 12 1

Stadt Wuppertal   Stadt Wuppertal

Stadt Wuppertal
Jugend und Freizeit

Freizeit- und Bildungsangebote 2004

Sehr geehrte Frau Schmidt,

Stadt Wuppertal
Jugend und Freizeit

Zwischen Sinn und Unsinn
Kunst und Kulturelles in Wuppertal

Januar 2004
Ausgabe/Heft Nr. 01
www.wuppertal.de

Stadt Wuppertal

Grün, grün, grün sind alle meine...
Umweltaktionen in und um Wuppertal

Januar 2004
Ausgabe/Heft Nr. 01
www.wuppertal.de

Stadt Wuppertal

Wo es lang geht und wo nicht
Straßen und Verkehr in Wuppertal

Januar 2004
Ausgabe/Heft Nr. 01
www.wuppertal.de

Stadt Wuppertal

Kunst und Kulturelles in Wuppertal
Meldestellen und Ämter in Wuppertal
Umweltaktionen in und um Wuppertal
Bergische Spezialitäten in Wuppertal
Straßen und Verkehr in Wuppertal

Stadt Wuppertal   Stadt Wuppertal   Stadt Wuppertal   Stadt Wuppertal   Stadt Wuppertal

01   02   03   04   05

Nominated for the
red dot: junior prize

TITLE
Stadt- und Bürger-
kommunikation:
Ein Corporate-Identity-
Konzept für die Stadt
Wuppertal

TYPE OF WORK
Undergraduate
dissertation

CLIENT
Bergische Universität
Wuppertal
Prof. Hans Günter
Schmitz
(supervising professor)

APPEARED IN
04|2004

DESIGN
Nicolas Markwald,
Wuppertal
Nina Neusitzer,
Wuppertal

RED DOT BEST OF THE BEST

RED DOT: BEST OF THE BEST

Mit der Ehrenauszeichnung „red dot: best of the best" (Höchste Designqualität) prämiert die international besetzte Jury Arbeiten, die außergewöhnlich hohen Ansprüchen an die gestalterische Qualität, den Innovationsgrad, die Ästhetik, den Gehalt und die Prägnanz genügen.
Die Auszeichnung vergibt das Design Zentrum Nordrhein Westfalen an die maximal drei besten Arbeiten der einzelnen Produktgruppen. Die insgesamt elf Gruppen umfassen Arbeiten aus den Bereichen Juniorpreis, Werbung, Unternehmenskommunikation, Produktkommunikation, Finanzkommunikation, Öffentlicher Raum, Wertdrucksachen, Fernsehen und AV-Medien, Kultur und Sport, Printkommunikation, Digitale Medien.
Unter 2.936 Einsendungen wählten die Jurorinnen und Juroren 31 Arbeiten aus, denen sie höchste Designqualität bescheinigten. Alle werden auf den folgenden Seiten dokumentiert.
Jean Jacques Schaffner, Frido Steinen-Broo und Stefan Ytterborn beurteilten die Kategorien Werbung, Produktkommunikation, Wertdrucksachen und Printkommunikation. Mervyn Kurlansky, Guy Schockaert und Kurt Weidemann jurierten die Bereiche Unternehmenskommunikation, Finanzkommunikation, Öffentlicher Raum sowie Kultur und Sport. Cristina Chiappini, Thomas Kurppa und Erich Sommer begutachteten die Kategorien Fernsehen und AV-Medien und Digitale Medien.

RED DOT: BEST OF THE BEST

"red dot: best of the best" (highest design quality) is a special award given by the international panel of judges to pieces of work that satisfy exceptionally high standards of design quality, innovation, aesthetics, content and succinctness.

Design Zentrum Nordrhein Westfalen gives this award to a maximum of three outstanding pieces of work in each product category. The eleven categories include work from the following areas: junior prize, advertising, corporate communication, product communication, financial communication, public areas, printed valuables, television and media, culture and sport, print communication, and digital media.

From the 2,936 items submitted, the judges selected 31 pieces of work which they felt satisfied the highest standards of design quality. These works have been documented in full on the following pages.

Jean Jacques Schaffner, Frido Steinen-Broo and Stefan Ytterborn assessed the advertising, product communication, printed valuables and print communication categories. Mervyn Kurlansky, Guy Schockaert and Kurt Weidemann judged the corporate communication, financial communication, public areas and culture and sport categories. Cristina Chiappini, Thomas Kurppa and Erich Sommer cast their critical eye over the television and media and digital media categories.

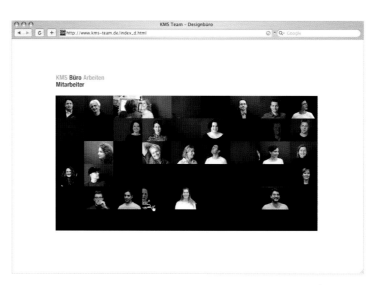

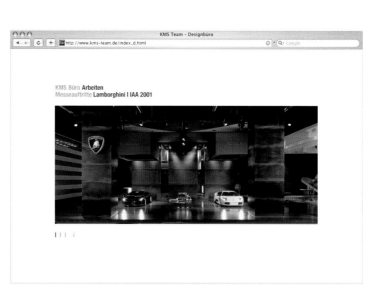

TITLE
www.kms-team.de

TYPE OF WORK
Website

DESIGN
KMS Team GmbH,
Munich
Creative direction:
Michael Keller,
Knut Maierhofer,
Christoph Rohrer
Art direction:
Bruno Marek
Text: Axel Sanjosé
Content management:
Bernd Müller
Project management:
Norman Müller

KMS Büro Arbeiten
Referenzen **Lamborghini I Produktlogo Murciélago**

Nach über zehn Jahren präsentierte Lamborghini mit dem »Murciélago« erstmals einen neuen Boliden, der auf der Frankfurter Automesse dem automobilen Mythos der Marke entsprechend inszeniert werden sollte. Um die Faszination der Fahrzeuge durch die bloße Präsenz zur Entfaltung kommen zu lassen, entfernten wir alles Überflüssige und Unstimmige. In dem abgegrenzten Raum gewannen die Fahrzeuge die Aura von Kult- gegenständen. Über ihnen thronte jeweils ein schwarzer Block mit ihrer Negativkontur – Material gewordene Symbole eines imaginierten Geburts- vorgangs. Die umgebenden baulichen Elemente wirkten kompakt und mächtig; die beherrschende Farbe war, von gelben Akzenten abgesehen, Schwarz. Die Großzügigkeit der Dimension, die strenge Linienführung und das archaisch wirkende Material (Stahl) strahlten Erhabenheit und Unabhängigkeit aus. Analog dazu hatten wir auch den Schriftzug des »Murciélago« einen monolithischen Charakter verliehen und dabei ein markantes Fahrzeugdetail aufgegriffen: die Lettern heben sich aus der Grundfläche heraus wie die Flanken des »Murciélago« während der Fahrt.

I I I i

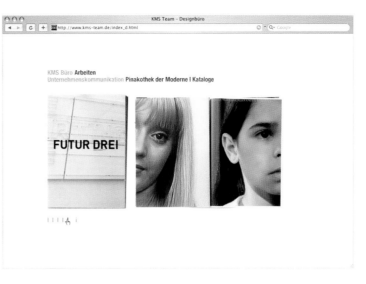

KMS Büro **Arbeiten**
Unternehmenskommunikation **Pinakothek der Moderne I Kataloge**

KMS Büro **Arbeiten**
Unternehmenskommunikation **Pinakothek der Moderne I Kataloge**

Das Museum vereint vier unabhängige Sammlungen der Bereiche Kunst, Graphik, Architektur und Design. Um diese Vielfalt nicht unzulässig zu verzerren, entschieden wir uns für einen reduzierten Umschlagentwurf, der nur den Namen und das Logo zeigt. Für den Hintergrund wählten wir eine Palette aus fünf Farbtönen für die einzelnen Sprachversionen. Beim Satz- spiegel legten wir die im Logo enthaltene Vierteilung als formales Prinzip zugrunde. Jeder der Sammlungen ist ein Viertel der Seitenfläche zugewiesen; im jeweiligen Kapitel werden dort die Abbildungen und die Bildlegenden positioniert.
Für die wechselnden Ausstellungen des Bereichs Gegenwartskunst war eine Zeitschrift zu konzi- pieren. Sie sollte ästhetisch auf höchstem Niveau stehen und zugleich die Rolle der Kunst als kritische, sich widersetzende gesellschaftliche Kraft widerspiegeln. Mit der Wahl des Formats (DIN A1) wird eine klare Botschaft vermittelt: Gegenwartskunst nimmt Raum in Anspruch, ist sperrig, lässt sich nicht klein kriegen. Gleichzeitig haben die großflächigen Fotos einen eigenen ästhetischen Reiz und lassen sich separat als Poster verwenden. Der von uns entwickelte Name FUTUR DREI ist als erfundene grammatikalische Form zu verstehen. Sie bezeichnet in Analogie zu Futur I (Zukunft) und Futur II (Vergangenheit der Zukunft) die »Vorvergangenheit der Zukunft« – nichts anderes also als die Gegenwart, aber als Bestandteil der Zukunft verstanden.

I I I I I

KMS Büro **Arbeiten**
Messeauftritte **Audi I IAA 1999**

I I

KMS Büro **Arbeiten**
Messeauftritte **o2 Germany I CeBIT 2003**

I I I I i

TITLE
Millenia Nova

TYPE OF WORK
Website/interactive

CLIENT
Universal Music GmbH,
Berlin

APPEARED IN
11|2002

DESIGN
Factor Product GmbH,
Munich
Axel Schildt,
Thomas Märkl

TITLE
Mission Statement

TYPE OF WORK
Image brochure

CLIENT
Accell, Braunlage

APPEARED IN
09|2003

DESIGN
Sign Kommunikation
GmbH, Frankfurt/Main

TITLE
Zanders ikono

TYPE OF WORK
Campaign

CLIENT
M-real Zanders GmbH,
Bergisch Gladbach

APPEARED IN
12|2003–04|2004

DESIGN
BRANDIT
Marketing und Kom-
munikation, Cologne
Peter Specht,
Petra Steuns

TITLE
Base Campaña 2004

TYPE OF WORK
Advertising magazine

CLIENT
Base Detall Sport SA,
Barcelona

APPEARED IN
2004

DESIGN
Ruiz + Company,
Barcelona

TITLE
Kunst klebt

TYPE OF WORK
Poster campaign

APPEARED IN
04|2004

DESIGN
Leitwerk
Büro für Kommuni-
kation, Cologne
Ilka Helmig
Photography:
Kerstin Vieg

TITLE
Jazz Festival
Willisau '03

TYPE OF WORK
Poster

CLIENT
Jazz in Willisau

APPEARED IN
08|2003

DESIGN
Niklaus Troxler Design,
Willisau
Prof. Niklaus Troxler

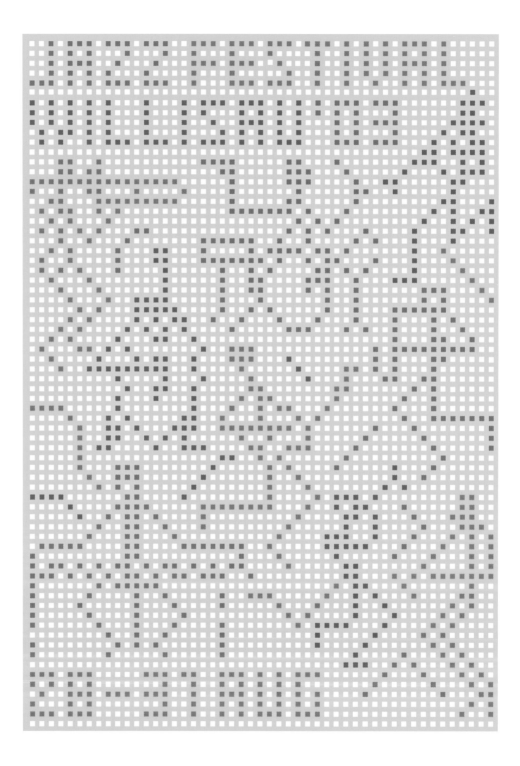

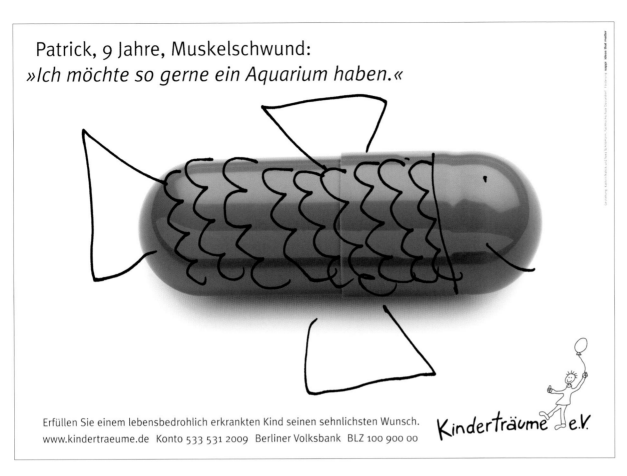

Patrick, 9 Jahre, Muskelschwund:
»Ich möchte so gerne ein Aquarium haben.«

Erfüllen Sie einem lebensbedrohlich erkrankten Kind seinen sehnlichsten Wunsch.
www.kindertraeume.de Konto 533 531 2009 Berliner Volksbank BLZ 100 900 00

TITLE
Kinderträume
(junior award)

TYPE OF WORK
Advertisements,
billboards, flyers,
postcard-set

CLIENT
Kinderträume e.V.,
Berlin

APPEARED IN
Decade 34|2003,
Decade 1|2004

DESIGN
Svea Schildmann,
Düsseldorf
Kathrin Nahlik,
Meerbusch

Anne, 8 Jahre, Leukämie:
»Ich möchte gerne in den Zoo.«

Erfüllen Sie einem lebensbedrohlich erkrankten Kind seinen sehnlichsten Wunsch.
www.kindertraeume.de Konto 533 531 2009 Berliner Volksbank BLZ 100 900 00

Sebastian, 7 Jahre, Knochenkrebs:
»Einmal mit der Feuerwehr fahren,
das wäre toll.«

Erfüllen Sie einem lebensbedrohlich erkrankten Kind seinen sehnlichsten Wunsch.
www.kindertraeume.de Konto 533 531 2009 Berliner Volksbank BLZ 100 900 00

TITLE
Ghostwriting

TYPE OF WORK
Business stationery

CLIENT
The Mission Group,
Stuttgart

APPEARED IN
06|2003

DESIGN
Leonhardt & Kern
Werbung GmbH,
Stuttgart
Armin Jochum,
Uli Weber,
Wolfgang Schif,
Michiko Schif

GHOST-WRITING FREELANCERS AT THE MISSION GROUP
BETTINA KRAMER GMBH
THEODOR-HEUSS-STRASSE 30, 70174 STUTTGART
TELEFON 0711/87 03 57 10, TELEFAX 0711/87 03 57 23

GHOST-WRITING FREELANCERS AT THE MISSION GROUP BETTINA KRAMER GMBH

TITLE
Das L&K Markenbuch

TYPE OF WORK
Brochure, album

APPEARED IN
12|2003

DESIGN
Leonhardt & Kern
Werbung GmbH,
Stuttgart
Uli Weber, Jörg Bauer

56

TITLE
Werte

TYPE OF WORK
Annual report
2002/2003

CLIENT
schlott gruppe AG,
Freudenstadt

DESIGN
strichpunkt, Stuttgart
Kirsten Dietz,
Jochen Radeker,
Stephanie Zehender

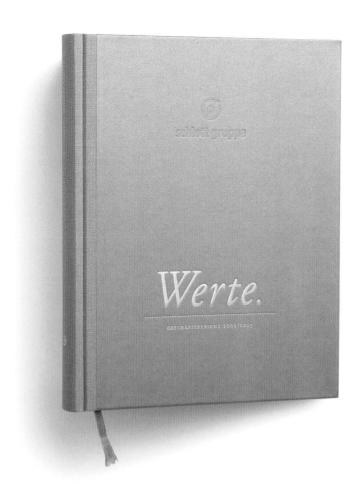

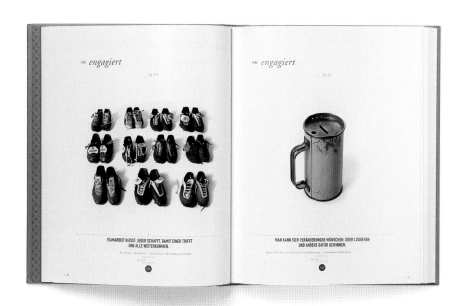

Bergbach

Kiesel

Wir folgten dem Bachlauf.

An einer ruhigeren Stelle,
zeichneten hinabhängende Zweige
feine Striche auf die Oberfläche.

»Jede Form«, sagte sie,
»entsteht aus Linien und Kreisen.«

Dann griff sie ei
und ließ ih

Weiden

Sandstein

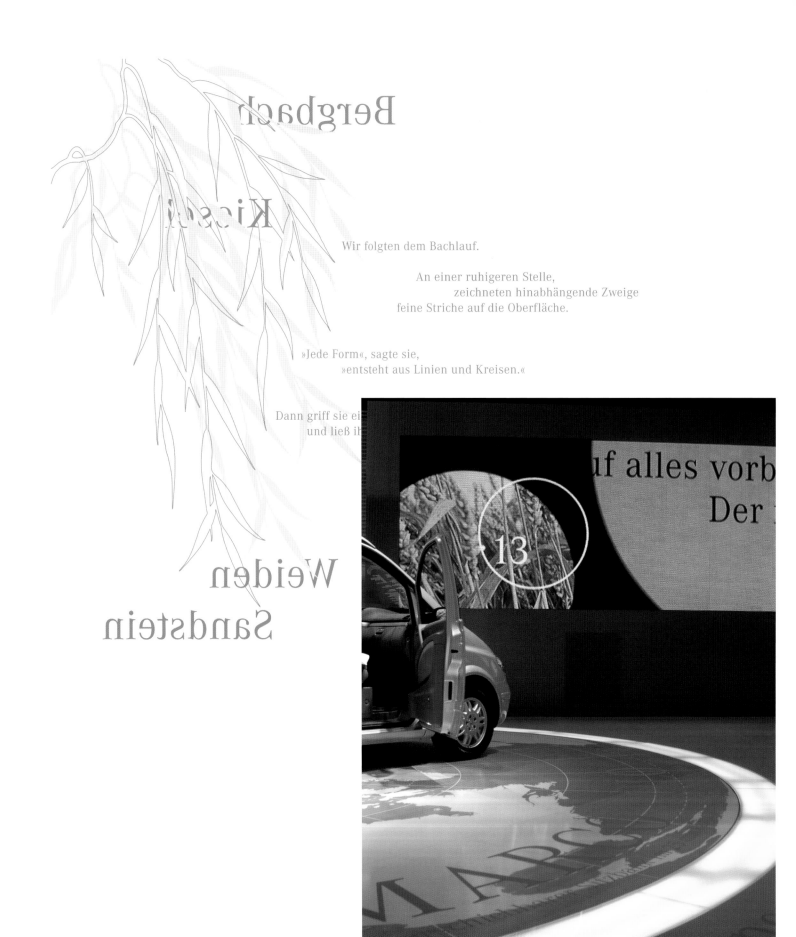

TITLE
Caravan Salon
Düsseldorf 2003

TYPE OF WORK
Trade fair
communication

CLIENT
DaimlerChrysler AG,
DCVD, Berlin
Nicole Florian

APPEARED IN
08|2003

DESIGN
Waidmann/Post,
Braunschweig
Stefan Waidmann,
Mechthild Post

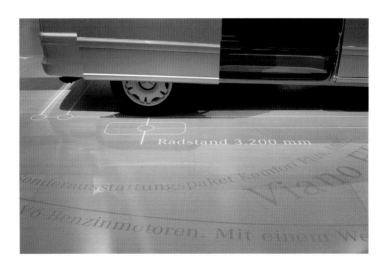

TITLE
Deutsches Hygiene-
Museum Dresden
(junior award)

TYPE OF WORK
Guidance system

CLIENT
Kulka & Partner
Architekten BDA,
Dresden

APPEARED IN
11|2003

DESIGN
Gourdin,
für Gestaltung,
Leipzig
Nathanaël Gourdin,
Klaus Hübner

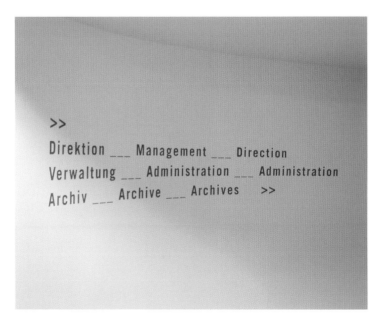

TITLE
.tif – Einflüsse neuer
Medien auf die
Fotokunst
(junior award)

TYPE OF WORK
Professional reference

CLIENT
Merz-Akademie,
Hochschule für
Gestaltung, Stuttgart

DESIGN
Peter Rummel,
Stuttgart
Angélique Bolter,
Stuttgart

TITLE
Information der
Hamburg School of
Entertainment

TYPE OF WORK
Brochure

CLIENT
Hamburg School of
Entertainment,
Hamburg

APPEARED IN
12|2003

DESIGN
Corporate Marketing,
Munich
Peter Aldag
Photography:
Esther Haase,
Hamburg

Die **Hamburg School of Entertainment** ist eine Fachschule für professionelles **Entertainment.** Zum Förderkreis der Hamburg School of Entertainment zählen neben der Trägergesellschaft StreLive Tivoli Entertainment & Consulting GmbH die Reederei Sietmaus, die Theater Schmidt und Schmidts Tivoli sowie die Freie und Hansestadt Hamburg. Zahlreiche Freunde und Gönner setzen sich ehrenamtlich und mit Begeisterung für die Belange der Schule und der Studierenden ein. **Die Schule ist eine nichtkommerzielle Institution, deren einziger Zweck die Ausbildung des künstlerischen Nachwuchses ist.** Der Lehrplan baut auf drei Bereichen, den Fächern Gesang, Tanz und Schauspiel, auf. Die Fächer werden einzeln und fachübergreifend studiert und erlernt. Auf das handwerkliche Rüstzeug legt die Schule großen Wert. Oberstes Studienziel ist die Herausbildung persönlicher Fähigkeiten wie Hingabe und Ausstrahlung. Die Schule wendet sich an junge, viel versprechende Talente, die eine ausgezeichnete Ausbildung mit viel Praxis anstreben. Das Studium dauert **Sechs Semester und endet für die erfolgreichen Absolventen mit dem Abschluss Musiktheaterdarsteller.**

5

Information
der Hamburg School of Entertainment
zum **Fachstudium Entertainment** mit Abschluss zum Musiktheaterdarsteller

Interdisziplinärer und integrativer Unterricht Für das Ausbildungsziel Entertainer werden die einzelnen Unterrichtsfächer Gesang, Tanz und Schauspiel zu einer Gesamtheit verknüpft. Erreicht wird dies durch einen fächerübergreifenden Unterricht und die enge Zusammenarbeit der Dozenten.

Technik und handwerkliches Können sind für den guten Entertainer eine unverzichtbare Basis. Daher müssen die Grundlagen in der Ausbildung im jeden Fach systematischer Bestandteil der Ausbildung. Neben der Technik sind es aber vor allem die persönlichen Fähigkeiten wie Leidenschaft, Spielfreude und Hingabe, welche Voraussetzung für eine besondere Ausstrahlung sind und den herausragenden Entertainer ausmachen. Die Studierenden entwickeln diese Fähigkeiten im Rahmen des Unterrichts in allen Fächern weiter.

Fachbereich Tanz

Das erste Jahr schafft die physischen und psychischen Grundlagen für die Anforderungen an einen tänzerischen Bühnenauftritt. Das tägliche Training setzt sich zusammen aus klassischem Ballett, Anatomie, Jazz und Sprungtraining, aber auch mentales Training zur Steigerung der Körperbeherrschung, Körperwahrnehmung, Entfaltung, Erweiterung und Verbesserung werden vermittelt. Die Ausbildung im klassischen Ballett beginnt bei den Grundlagen der Ballettelemente an der Stange und im freien Raum. Sie wird in den folgenden Schuljahren in ihrer Gesamtheit erweitert. Im ersten Jahr erlernen die Studierenden die einzelnen Elemente der klassischen Tanztechnik, Grundschritt und Koordination sowie ein tänzerisches Grundrepertoire. Das zweite Schuljahr vertieft die bisher erworbenen Kenntnisse und Techniken. Die Studierenden nehmen an Intensivtanzstunden teil, in welchen sie selbstständig diverse Stile, Paartanz oder Choreographien entwickeln können. Der Unterricht wird um das Fach Modern Jazz erweitert. Das Abschlussjahr professionalisiert die Bereiche klassisches Ballett und Jazz. Neben Kombinationen und einzelige Grundübungen erlernen werden. Im Balletttraining konzentriert sich auf neue Tanzserien und Sprünge, sodass im letzten Schuljahr die einzelnen Tanzstunden in Workshops und Probearbeit perfektioniert werden.

11

Das Herzstück der Hamburg School of Entertainment ist der große Tanzsaal. Die ehemalige Festhalle der Schramberger Unterrichts ist komplett mit Parkettschwingboden ausgelegt. Der Saal verfügt über eine ausgefeilte Theatertechnik aus Bühne, Licht und Ton, über eine große Spiegelwand und viel Tageslicht, sowie die nötigen Aufwärmräume erhält, die zum Tanzbereich zählen.

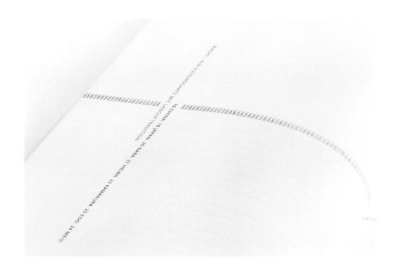

TITLE
Washi – Tradition
und Kunst des Japan-
papiers
(junior award)

TYPE OF WORK
Two volumes in
slipcase

APPEARED IN
09|2003

DESIGN
mikan – Mariko Takagi,
Düsseldorf

TITLE
Typeschnittstelle Flow
(junior award)

TYPE OF WORK
Type design, book
design, poster design

APPEARED IN
01|2004

DESIGN
Martina Kurz,
Stuttgart

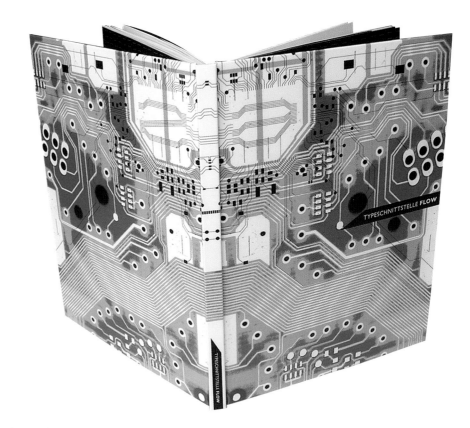

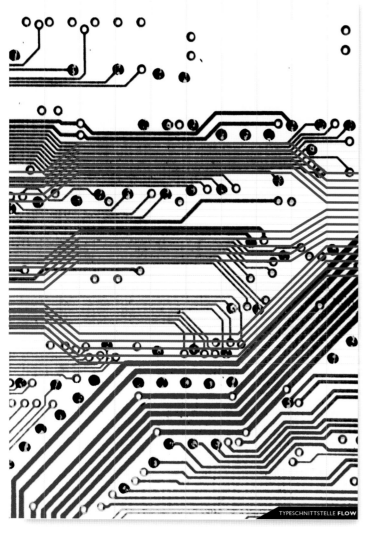

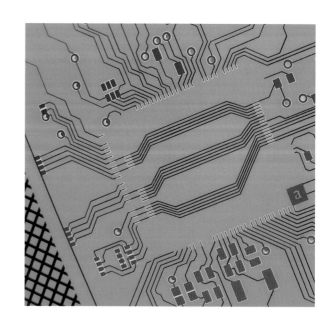

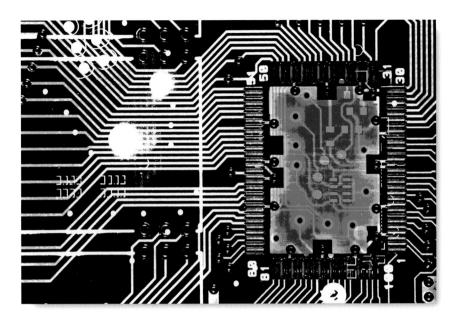

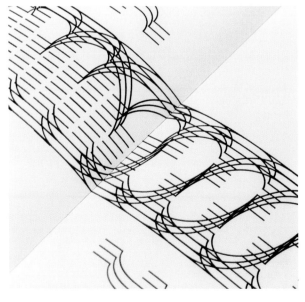

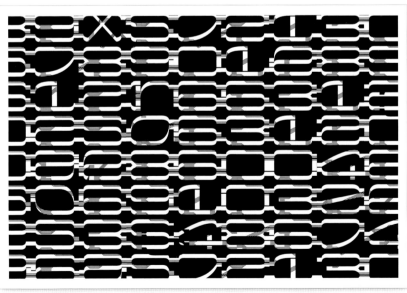

71

TITLE
The Light on Your
Face Warms My Heart

TYPE OF WORK
Book design

CLIENT
Edition Patrick Frey

APPEARED IN
05|2004

DESIGN
Büro4
Gestaltung und
Kommunikation,
Zurich

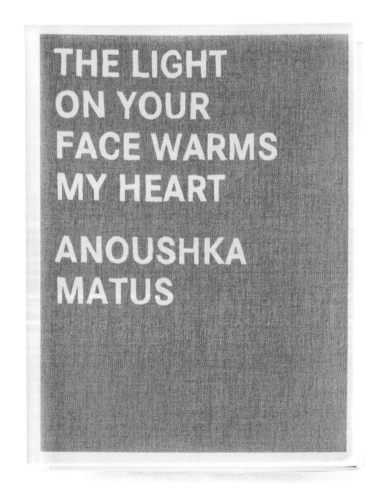

ISBN 3-905509-50-4

Dear Anoushka,
The night outside is so dark and quiet. So wonderfully quiet. Everyone's asleep and the lights are out. Except one of my neighbours who is ironing and watching TV. Actually, he does that all the time: irons and watches TV. Once he took a pistol apart and cleaned it and watched TV at the same time. But usually he's ironing. I don't see a big difference between ironing shirts and cleaning pistols. There goes my peace and quiet. Thanks to a Peugeot. A souped-up blue 305. Racing past my window at least 60 mph, the street lights gliding and jerking on the high-gloss enamel. And then he slams on the brakes, screeching to a halt at a red light that's not far away. He's done it four times in a row and I'm sure he's going to be back.

I'm sitting barefoot in the kitchen at my computer at this late hour because I'm writing the postscript for your book. I'm making an effort because I don't want the postscript to sound as if it was in an art catalogue, as that's not what your book deserves. Your book deserves a postscript that's really something. A postscript that blows your mind. A postscript as strong as Mr. Spock's hold. Yeah, I know: that's a hard act to follow.

So here I am sitting in the kitchen and I remember that I thought of something last week when I was in Greenwich on business (no, it was not an interview with the Cutty Sark, but something of that nature). I remembered how we'd walked over the hill from Lewisham years ago to take the tunnel under the Thames in Greenwich. Remember? We'd been visiting your aunt in her house with a great garden in the back. How many years ago was it? So we walked over the hill from Lewisham and we sang the song 'It's just an illusion' by Imagination, but we didn't sing 'It's just an illusion' but 'It's just one from Lewisham' or something like that. It was a gorgeous day and you were wearing a T-shirt I had bought for you in London the day before. A T-shirt with an ironic saying on it that I never saw you wear again. I didn't know yet that you thought printed T-shirts were dumb (which it's taken me all this time to understand because printed T-shirts really are dumb – hey, it took me 35 years to figure that out).

When I was in Greenwich again last week, years later, and I saw the park again, I remembered how we sat on the grass in the sun watching Indian families picnicking and barely being able to control their kids, and you were drawing. I don't remember what you were drawing, whether it was a tree or the children playing or a stray dog. But you were drawing. As you often does.

And it occurred to me that you were actually always drawing. No matter what situation comes to mind: I picture you drawing. You would draw in front of the TV (do you remember how we used to watch TV Nation? That report on the least visited state in the USA? Where there were only snowplows and kids in bulky parkas who were bored to death? And wasn't that where the Bowling Hall of Fame was?). At the movies. Drinking coffee after going shopping on Saturdays. Eating at a restaurant. Visiting my parents (or rather, the one time we visited them). On the Ferris wheel.

You were always drawing. Okay, not always. Nobody can always be drawing. But you certainly did it an awful lot. A lot more than average. If there was a list titled 'cool people who spend an above average time drawing' in the book 'Everything You Need to Know', you'd probably be pretty near the top of the list.

TITLE
Jüdisches Museum
Berlin

TYPE OF WORK
Annual report
2001/2002

CLIENT
Stiftung Jüdisches
Museum Berlin

APPEARED IN
06|2003

DESIGN
Groothuis, Lohfert,
Consorten, Hamburg
Veronika Grigkar
Production:
Ralf Schnarrenberger,
Tanja Siebenhaar

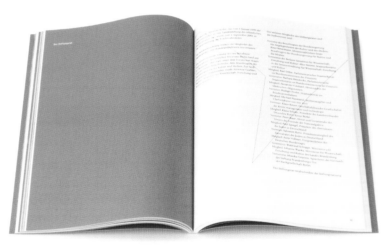

TITLE
Einsechsundzwanzig-
buchstabenbuch

TYPE OF WORK
Book

CLIENT
Hatje Cantz Verlag,
Ostfildern

DESIGN
Barbara + Gerd
Baumann,
Schwäbisch Gmünd

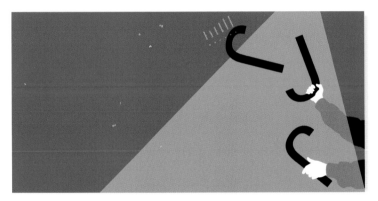

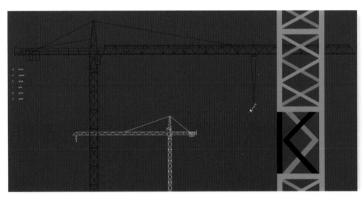

TITLE
Experience new
Sesame Street.

TYPE OF WORK
Promotional
campaign

CLIENT
Sesame Street
Partners Japan, Tokyo

APPEARED IN
03|2004

DESIGN
ASATSU-DK INC, Tokyo
Yukimi Sano

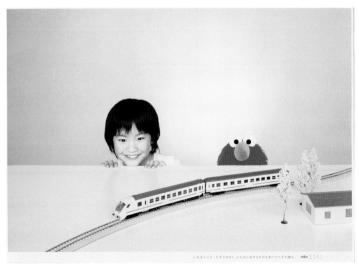

TITLE
SAL magazine

TYPE OF WORK
Cover art

CLIENT
Daiichi Kosho Co., Ltd.,
Tokyo

APPEARED IN
2002–2004

DESIGN
Hideki Inaba Design,
Tokyo
Hideki Inaba

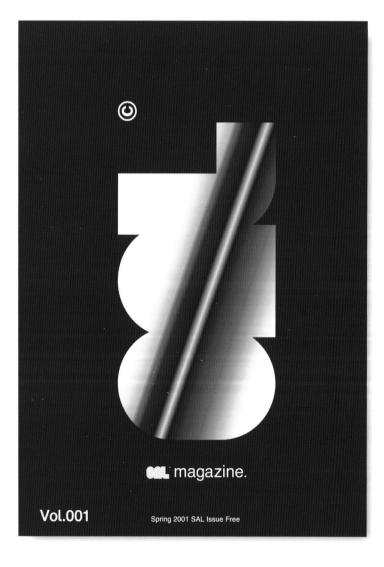

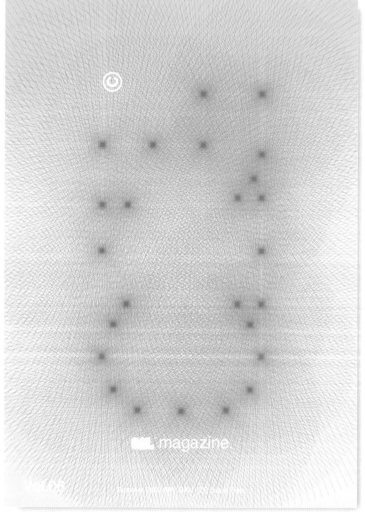

SAL magazine.

Vol.05 Spring 2002 RE:NEWAL Issue Free

SAL magazine
Vol.10
'AUDIOVISUAL'
Free Winter 2003
小山田圭吾 辻川幸一
郎 黒川良一 明鏡止
水 宇川直宏 寺田創
一 小松好幸 藤本
"ANI" 健太郎 ジョニ
ー・ハードスタッフ
エアサイド バー
ンストーマーズ 今井
トゥーンズ 稲葉英樹

SAL

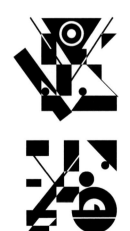

SAL magazine
Vol.09 'Drop' Free
Summer 2003
黒川知希 宇川直宏
江田龍介 秋田昌
美 千原航 氷見こず
え 黒田潔 ナン 稲
葉英樹

SAL New

TITLE
Bewerbung zur
Kulturhauptstadt

TYPE OF WORK
Book

CLIENT
Kulturreferat Stadt
Augsburg

DESIGN
Factor Design AG,
Hamburg
Johannes Erler,
Jindrich Novotny

Warum Augsburg bei der künstlerischen Gestaltung des Stadtraumes auf die Mitwirkung von Bürgerinnen und Bürgern setzt.

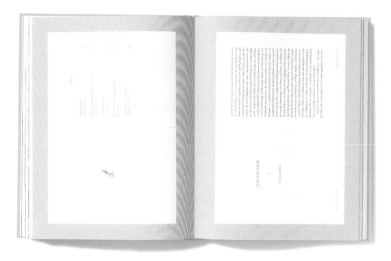

Wie sich Gesellschaft gegenüber dem Genie verhält und wie sich das Genie gegenüber der Gesellschaft verhält.

Wie die Industriestadt Augsburg nach Europa hinauswirkt.

TITLE
La Tarde –
Der Nachmittag
(junior award)

TYPE OF WORK
Book

CLIENT
Fachhochschule Mainz
Prof. Ulysses Voelker
(supervising professor)

APPEARED IN
02|2004

DESIGN
Irene Mohr,
Linnig Partners
commerce communi-
cations GmbH

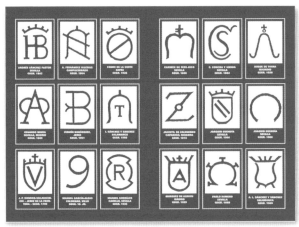

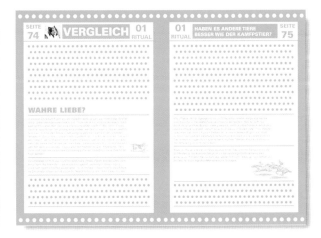

«Cargar la suerte» bedeutet, das Manöver laden. Dabei setzt man den Fuß nach vorne, an dessen Seite der Stier vorbei soll.

Durch die kunstvollen Schwenks wird das Temperament des Tiers gemäßigt. Der Stier ist von diesem bewegten Tuch regelrecht fasziniert. Er hält es für den vermeintlichen Feind. Der Kreativität des Toreros sind hier keine Grenzen gesetzt. Jeder hat seinen eigenen Stil und erfindet bestimmte, neue zusätzliche Elemente, die ihn kennzeichnen und zu seiner Marke werden.

Veronica   Revolera   1/2 Veronica

»CAPEAS«

Die Schwenks mit den Capas sind der verspielteste Teil einer Corrida und ohne jegliche Gewalt. Sie sind überwiegend im ersten Teil des Stierkampfs vorhanden. Die Capas sind die Verteidigung der Toreros und gleichzeitig Mittel, um den Stier von einem Ort zum anderen zu bringen. Dies wird in Form von pirouettenhaften Drehungen vollbracht.

Im Moment des Angriffs ist das Bein des Toreros nach vorne geschritten. Der Stier sieht sich nun gezwungen, seine gerade Anlaufsbahn zu verlassen und der Capa zu folgen.

SEITE 68 02 KUNST

02 KUNST SEITE 69

RED DOT DIGITAL MEDIA

RED DOT: DIGITAL MEDIA

Gewinner des erstmals vergebenen Sonderpreises „red dot: digital media" ist die interaktive Installation „floating.numbers", die das Unternehmen ART+COM für eine Sonderausstellung des Jüdischen Museums in Berlin realisiert hat.

Zentrales Element dieser Installation ist ein neun Meter langer und zwei Meter breiter interaktiver Tisch ähnlich einem überdimensionalen Touchscreen. Hunderte von Zahlen schwimmen auf seiner Oberfläche. Nach dem Zufallsprinzip tauchen aus diesem Zahlenstrom einzelne Ziffern auf. Sobald die Besucher diese berühren, offenbaren sie ihre Bedeutung – in Form von Texten, Bildern, Filmen und Animationen. Spielerisch und informativ zugleich erschließen sich den Besuchern die Zusammenhänge der Zeichen im Kontext von religiöser Tradition und moderner Welt.

Konzeption, Gestaltung und Realisierung stammen von ART+COM, Idee und Inhalt von Hürlimann + Lepp Ausstellungen. Das Designstudio ART+COM,1988 gegründet und mit Sitz in Berlin, entwickelt innovative Lösungen für neue Medien. Die Produkte und Installationen findet man im Internet, in Museen, Showrooms, Visitor- und Science-Centern sowie auf Messen und Events. Die Kunden kommen sowohl aus der Industrie als auch aus Forschung und Kultur: www.artcom.de.

The inaugural "red dot: digital media" has been awarded to the interactive installation "floating.numbers" from the company Art+Com for a special exhibition staged by the Jewish Museum in Berlin.

A central element of this installation is a nine metre long and two metre wide interactive table similar to a giant touchscreen with hundreds of numbers swimming on its surface. Single digits suddenly appear out of this datastream. As soon as the visitor touches one of these, it reveals its connotation – in the form of text, images, films or animation. Simultaneously playful and informative, the significance of the numbers is revealed to the visitors in the context of religious tradition and the modern world.

Conception, design and realization was in the hands of ART+COM. The idea and concept originates from the Hürlimann + Lepp exhibition. The design studio, ART+COM, founded in 1988 and located in Berlin, develops innovative solutions for new media. Their products and installations can be seen in the internet, or at museums, showrooms, visitor and science centres as well as trade exhibitions and events. Their customers range from industrial companies to research institutes and cultural organizations: www.artcom.de.

TITLE
floating.numbers –
Das Universum der
Zahlen

TYPE OF WORK
Interactive installation

CLIENT
Jüdisches Museum
Berlin

APPEARED IN
2004

DESIGN
ART + COM AG, Berlin

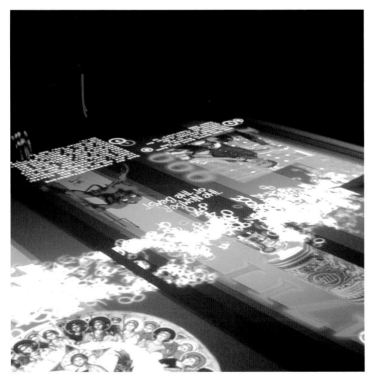

RED DOT DIGITALE MEDIEN
Werbebanner I Interstitials I E-Mail-Marketing I Digitale Nachschlagewerke
Trainings- und Lernsoftware I Digitale Corporate Identity I Animationen I Sonstiges
Online: Internetauftritte I Online-Spiele I Interface Design
Offline: CD-ROMs I CD-Is I DVDs I Kiosk-Systeme I Interfaces

RED DOT DIGITAL MEDIA
Advertising Banners | Interstitials | E-Mail Marketing | Digital Reference Works
Training and Educational Software | Digital Corporate Identity | Animations | Others
Online: Websites, Online Games, Interface Design
Offline: CD-ROMs | CD-Is | DVDs | Kiosk Systems | Interfaces

Jury:
Cristina Chiappini
Thomas Kurppa
Erich Sommer

TITLE

Digitale Medien/Inter-
media
www.muthesius.de/dmi

TYPE OF WORK

Website

APPEARED IN

10|2003

DESIGN

Muthesius Hochschule
Kiel
Felix Schultze, Guido v.
Schneider-Marientreu,
Florian Zöllner

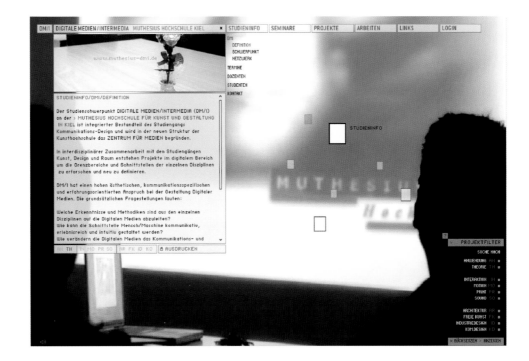

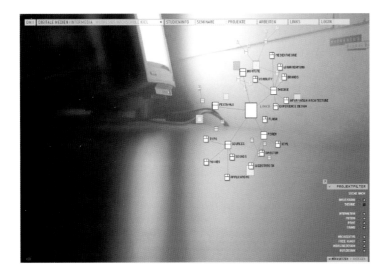

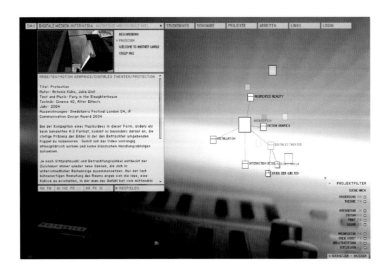

TITLE
www.eisfink.de

TYPE OF WORK
Website

CLIENT
Eisfink GmbH & Co.
KG, Ludwigsburg

APPEARED IN
02|2004

DESIGN
Werbewelt Inter-
active GmbH,
Ludwigsburg
Wolfgang Benz

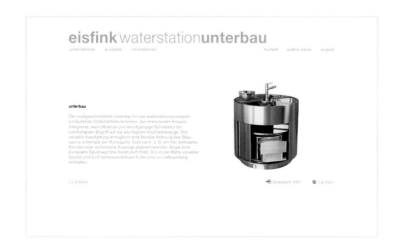

TITLE
Barrierefreier Relaunch
Internetauftritt Kölner
Philharmonie
www.koelner-philhar-
monie.de

TYPE OF WORK
Website

CLIENT
Kölner Philharmonie/
KölnMusik GmbH,
Cologne

APPEARED IN
06|2004

DESIGN
m.i.r. media, Cologne
Oliver Priester,
Eva-Maria Schreiner

TITLE
www.julia1926.net
(junior award)

TYPE OF WORK
Website

APPEARED IN
08|2003

DESIGN
HELTERSK3LTER.net,
Johannes Weymann

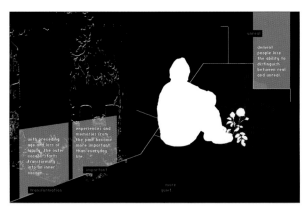

TITLE
HansPaetsch.de

TYPE OF WORK
Website

CLIENT
Hamster & James
h.n.c., London
BMG Ariola Classics
GmbH, Munich

APPEARED IN
03|2003

DESIGN
Die Firma GmbH,
Wiesbaden
Marco Fischer,
Susa Wilhelm,
Andreas Baier,
Tomasz Sawicki

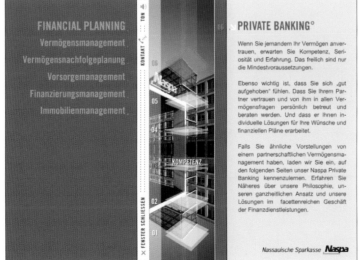

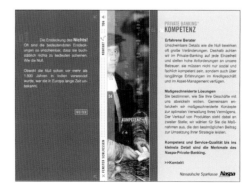

TITLE
Naspa.de

TYPE OF WORK
Internet portal

CLIENT
Nassauische Sparkasse,
Wiesbaden

APPEARED IN
03|2003

DESIGN
Die Firma GmbH,
Wiesbaden
Marco Fischer,
Susa Wilhelm,
Jochen Fritz,
Tomasz Sawicki

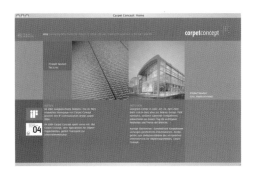

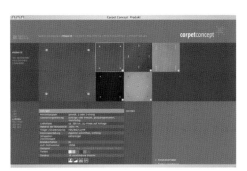

TITLE
Carpet Concept
Website 2004
www.carpet-concept.de

TYPE OF WORK
Website

CLIENT
Carpet Concept
Objekt-Teppichboden
GmbH, Bielefeld

APPEARED IN
02|2004

DESIGN
Projekttriangle,
Stuttgart
Danijela Djokic,
Martin Grothmaak,
Jürgen Späth
Conception:
Büro Blank,
Holzgerlingen

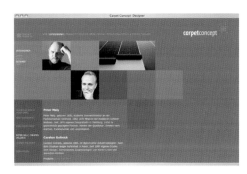

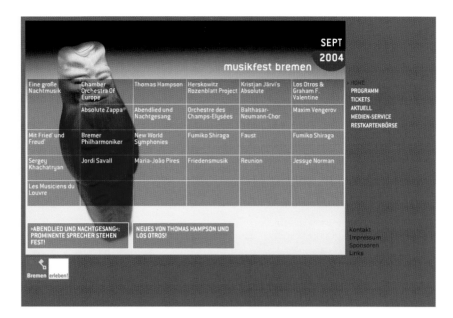

TITLE
www.musikfest-
bremen.de

TYPE OF WORK
Website

CLIENT
Musikfest Bremen
GmbH, Bremen

APPEARED IN
05|2003 – 06|2003

DESIGN
kleiner und bold
GmbH, Berlin
Cornelia Heinen

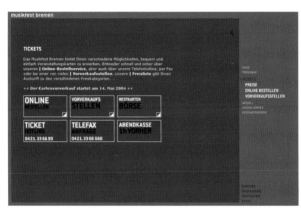

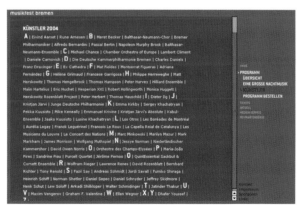

TITLE
Jan Kath Website

TYPE OF WORK
Website

CLIENT
Jan Kath GmbH,
Bochum

APPEARED IN
03|2003

DESIGN
Oktober Kommunika-
tionsdesign GmbH,
Bochum
Silke Löhmann,
René Wynands

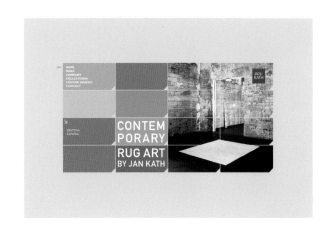

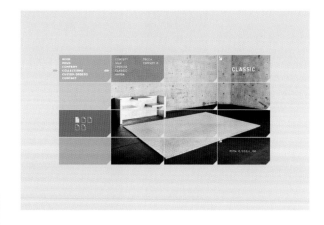

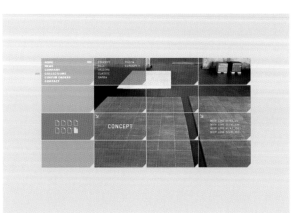

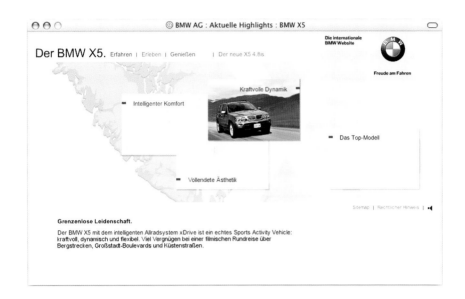

TITLE
Der BMW X5. Erfahren.
Erleben. Genießen.
www.bmw.com/x5

TYPE OF WORK
Website for product
launch

CLIENT
BMW AG, Munich

APPEARED IN
09|2003

DESIGN
BBDO InterOne GmbH,
Hamburg

TITLE
Cool Flame – The Game
www.be-the-first-
one.com

TYPE OF WORK
Online game for the
launch of the BMW 1
series

CLIENT
BMW AG, Munich

APPEARED IN
01|2004

DESIGN
BBDO InterOne GmbH,
Hamburg

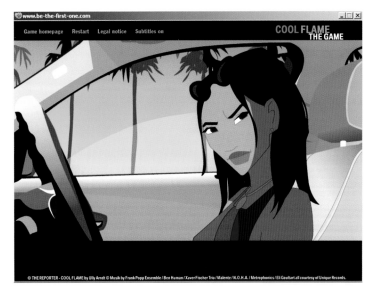

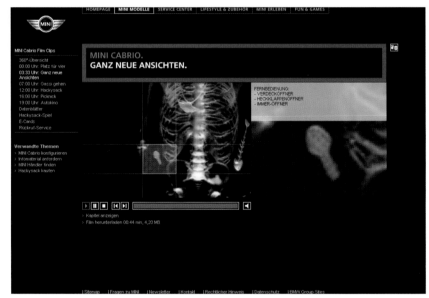

TITLE
MINI Cabrio
www.mini.com/cabrio

TYPE OF WORK
Internet special

CLIENT
BMW AG
Brand Communication
MINI, Munich

APPEARED IN
03 | 2004

DESIGN
BBDO InterOne
GmbH, Hamburg

TITLE
The Inside Story –
Der neue Volvo S40
www.volvocars.de/s40

TYPE OF WORK
Website

CLIENT
Volvo Car Germany
GmbH, Cologne

APPEARED IN
02|2004

DESIGN
Forsman & Bodenfors,
Göteborg

TITLE
www.toca-me.com
(junior award)

TYPE OF WORK
Website

CLIENT
TOCA ME GmbH,
Munich

APPEARED IN
01|2003

DESIGN
TOCA ME GmbH,
Munich
Nina Schmid,
Ronald Iberl,
Thorsten Iberl

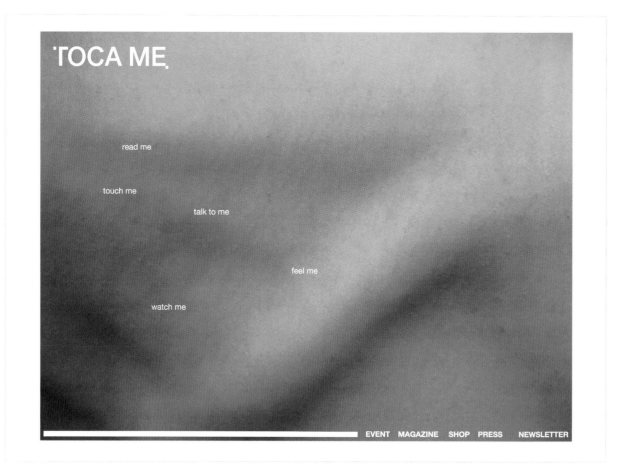

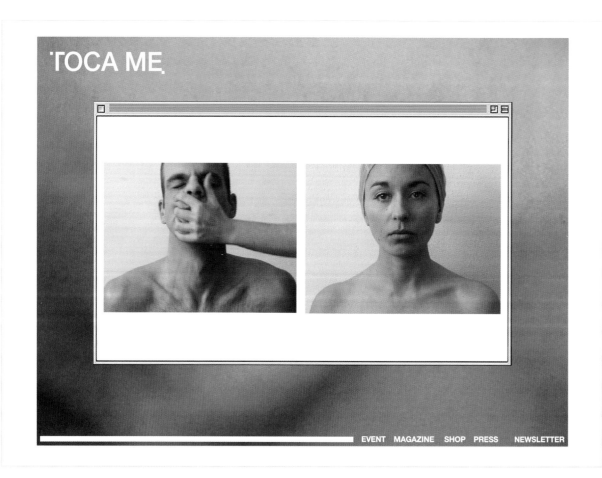

TITLE
Panasonic web
guidelines Europe

TYPE OF WORK
Website

CLIENT
Panasonic Deutsch-
land GmbH, Hamburg

APPEARED IN
02|2004

DESIGN
de-construct, London

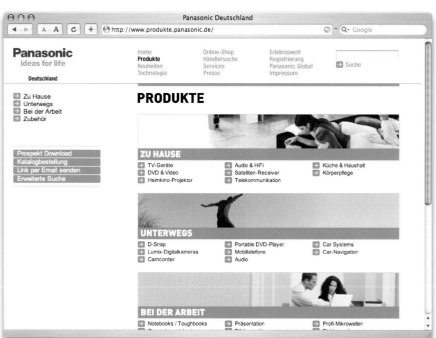

TITLE
Botanic Channel –
interactice DVD
installation on the
subject of psycho-
active plants
(junior award)

TYPE OF WORK
Interactive DVD for
kiosk system

CLIENT
Botanical Museum
Berlin-Dahlem,
FU Berlin

APPEARED IN
04|2004

DESIGN
FH Potsdam,
Goldener Westen
Toby Mory,
Daniel Becker,
Moritz Koepp,
Prof. Klaus Dufke
(supervising professor)

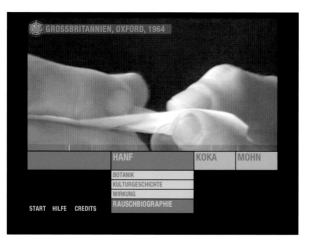

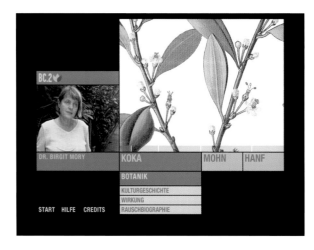

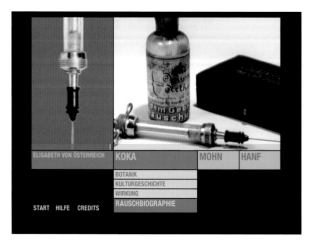

TITLE
www.one-silly.de

TYPE OF WORK
Website

CLIENT
ONe – the functional
drink GmbH & Co KG,
Salzburg

APPEARED IN
12|2003

DESIGN
Jung von Matt / Elbe
GmbH, Hamburg
Michael Kutschinski,
Elke Klinkhammer,
Christoph Behm,
Andre Wischnewski,
Daniel Mautz,
Marc Seibert,
Sergei Ivanov

TITLE
Model Team Hamburg

TYPE OF WORK
Website

CLIENT
Model Team, Hamburg

APPEARED IN
08|2003

DESIGN
REVORM, Hamburg
Claas Blüher,
Robert Siegmund

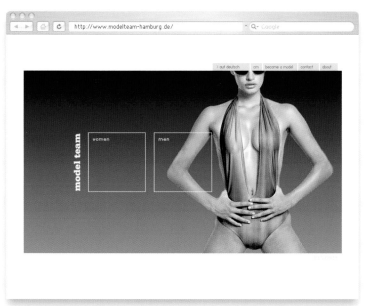

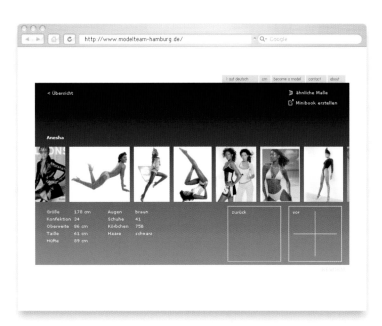

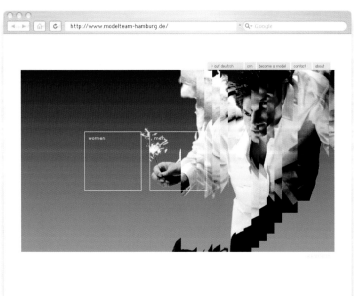

TITLE
Prinect

TYPE OF WORK
User interface design

DESIGN
Heidelberger
Druckmaschinen AG,
Heidelberg
Thomas Emig,
Volkhard Franke

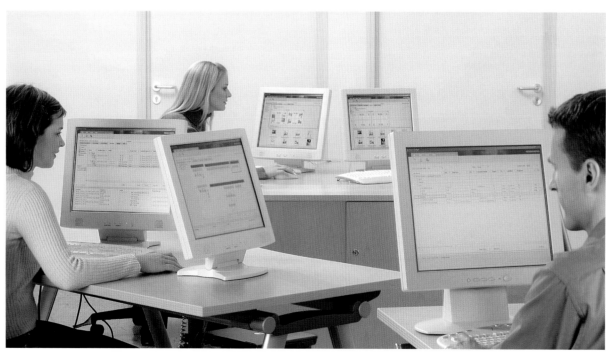

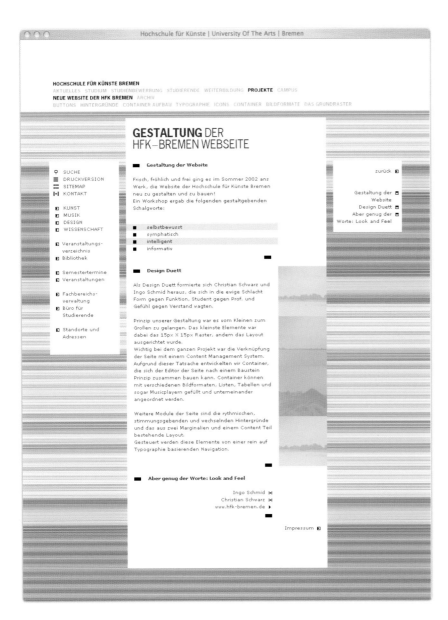

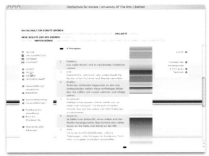

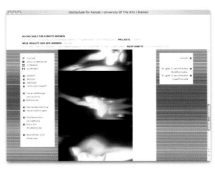

TITLE
Internetauftritt HfK
Bremen
(junior award)

TYPE OF WORK
Screen design

CLIENT
Hochschule für
Künste Bremen

APPEARED IN
11|2003

DESIGN
Ingo Schmid, Bremen
Christian Schwarz,
Bremen
Supported by the
project team

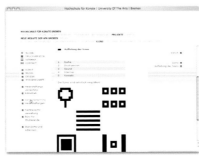

TITLE
Mixed Tape

TYPE OF WORK
Music platform

CLIENT
Mercedes-Benz,
Stuttgart

APPEARED IN
06|2004

DESIGN
Scholz & Volkmer
GmbH, Wiesbaden

TITLE
ECM Records Website

TYPE OF WORK
Website

CLIENT
ECM Records,
Gräfelfing

APPEARED IN
02|2004

DESIGN
Atelier
Bernd Kuchenbeiser,
Munich
Andreas Alber,
Bernd Kuchenbeiser

February 2004   www.ecmrecords.com

TITLE
DVD "Porsche Driving Academy"

TYPE OF WORK
DVD, promotional movies

CLIENT
Pon's Automobiel-handel, Leusden

APPEARED IN
2003

DESIGN
QuA Associates BV, Amsterdam

TITLE
Merten Website

TYPE OF WORK
Website

CLIENT
Merten GmbH & Co.
KG, Wiehl

APPEARED IN
04|2004

DESIGN
METADESIGN AG,
Berlin
Thomas Klein,
Anett Wagner,
Ulla Selmer
Web programming:
Christoph Kasmeridis,
Lutz Möbius

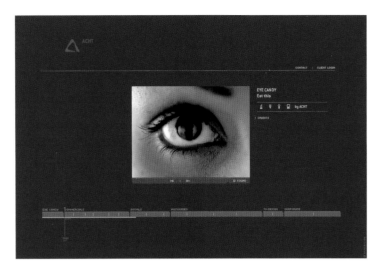
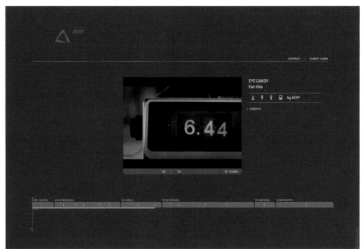
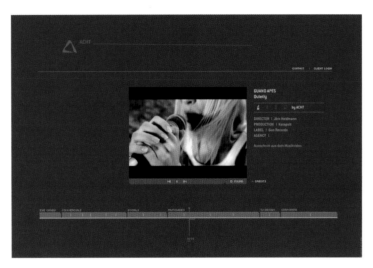

TITLE
Website Acht
Frankfurt

TYPE OF WORK
Website

CLIENT
Acht Frankfurt
digital solutions,
Frankfurt/Main

DESIGN
Scholz & Volkmer
GmbH, Wiesbaden

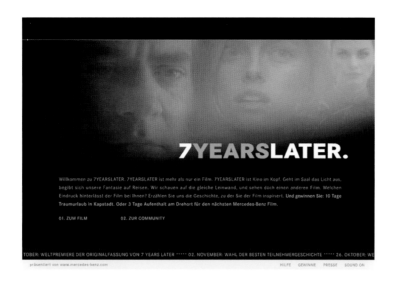

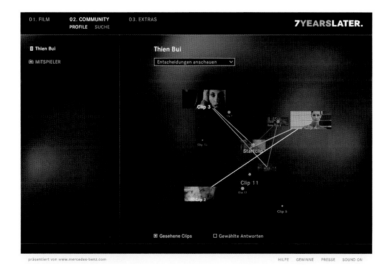

TITLE
Mercedes-Benz
"7 Years Later"

TYPE OF WORK
Website

CLIENT
Mercedes-Benz,
Stuttgart

APPEARED IN
09|2003

DESIGN
Scholz & Volkmer
GmbH, Wiesbaden

TITLE
VDW Award 04

TYPE OF WORK
Presentation of an
advertising film
award

CLIENT
VdW Verband
deutscher Werbefilm-
produzenten e.V.,
Hamburg

APPEARED IN
04|2004

DESIGN
Group.IE GmbH,
Frankfurt/Main
Kai Bergmann

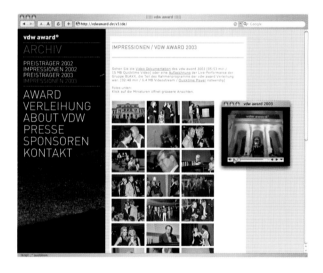

118

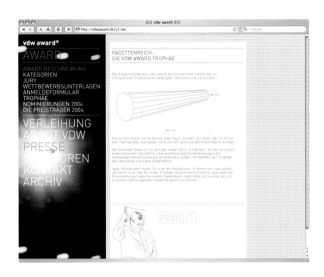

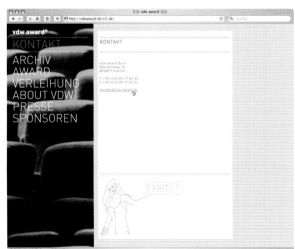

RED DOT FERNSEHEN | AV-MEDIEN
TV-On-Air-Promotion | TV-Design | Musikvideos | Sonstiges

RED DOT TELEVISION | MEDIA
TV On-Air Promotion | TV Design | Music Videos | Others

Jury:
Cristina Chiappini
Thomas Kurppa
Erich Sommer

TITLE
Karl Bartos
"I'm the message"

TYPE OF WORK
Music video

CLIENT
Home Records,
Hamburg
Sony Music, Berlin

APPEARED IN
09|2003

DESIGN
Direction:
Lucas Buchholz,
Bernd Brink
weissraum.de(sign),
Hamburg
Animation:
Florian Bruchhaeuser
Editing:
Aram Coen

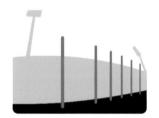

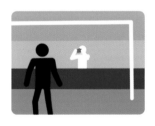

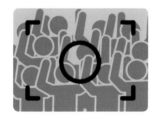
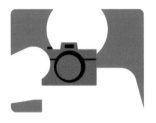

TITLE
Christian Kreuz
"Wir sind bereit"

TYPE OF WORK
Music video

CLIENT
Motor Music/
A division of Universal
Music GmbH, Berlin

APPEARED IN
04|2004

DESIGN
Designliga, Munich
Andreas Döhring,
Sasa Stanojcic,
Amir Sufi

RED DOT WERBUNG
Publikums-, Fach- und Tageszeitungsanzeigen | Plakate | Poster
Dialogmarketing (Mailings und Anzeigen) | Verkaufsförderung: Promotions | VKF-Material | Beilagen | Folder | Sonderaktionen
Text: Anzeigen | Mailings | Promotions | Plakate | Sonstiges
Funk-Spots | TV-Spots | Kinowerbefilme

RED DOT ADVERTISING

Advertisements in Trade Journals and Daily Newspapers | Billboards | Posters

Dialogue Marketing (Mailshots and Advertisements) | Sales Promotion: Promotions | Sales Materials | Inserts

Folders | Special Campaigns | Text: Advertisements, Mailshots | Promotions | Posters | Others

Radio Commercials | TV Spots | Cinema Commercials

Jury:
Jean Jacques Schaffner
Frido Steinen-Broo
Stefan Ytterborn

TITLE
Hände

TYPE OF WORK
Poster

CLIENT
Unsere kleinen Brüder
und Schwestern,
Karlsruhe

APPEARED IN
11|2003

DESIGN
Leonhardt & Kern
Werbung GmbH,
Stuttgart
Armin Jochum,
Thomas Schöllhorn,
Michael Kusterer,
J. Baldauf

VERY, VERY, VERY FAST
ASIA GOURMET-IMBISS

STUTTGARTER STRASSE 35 70469 STUTTGART FEUERBACH

HALLO YAMYAM TSCHÜSS.

TITLE
Schneller essen

TYPE OF WORK
Poster

CLIENT
GOI Fast Asia
Gourmet, Stuttgart

APPEARED IN
12|2003

DESIGN
Leonhardt & Kern
Werbung GmbH,
Stuttgart
Armin Jochum,
Thomas Schöllhorn,
Marc Oehlcke,
Wolfgang Schif

KOMM SCHLEMM FREU.

NI HAO KAUKAU VERDAUDAU.

TITLE
Erst 1 ... dann 2 ...
dann 3 ... dann 4!

TYPE OF WORK
Christmas cards

CLIENT
Ottenwälder und
Ottenwälder,
Schwäbisch Gmünd

APPEARED IN
12|2003

DESIGN
Ottenwälder und
Ottenwälder,
Schwäbisch Gmünd

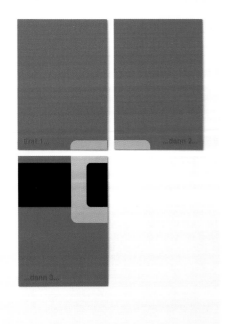

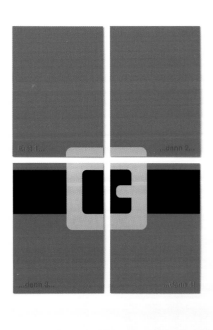

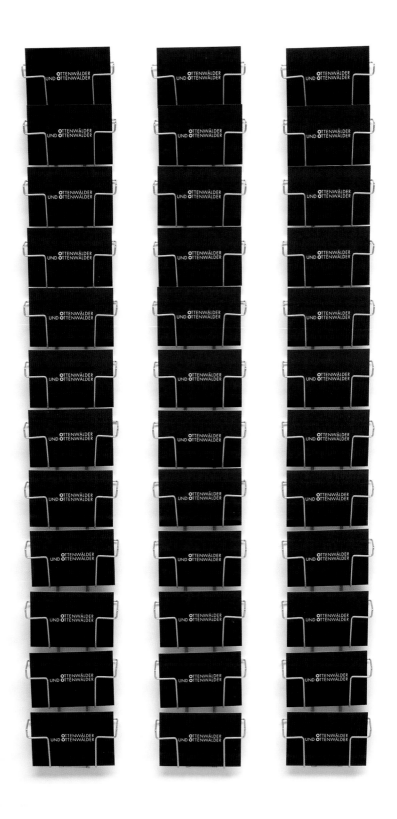

TITLE
Freikarten

TYPE OF WORK
Postcards

CLIENT
Ottenwälder und
Ottenwälder,
Schwäbisch Gmünd

APPEARED IN
10|2003

DESIGN
Ottenwälder und
Ottenwälder,
Schwäbisch Gmünd

TITLE
O und O – Mobile

TYPE OF WORK
Christmas card

CLIENT
Ottenwälder und
Ottenwälder,
Schwäbisch Gmünd

APPEARED IN
12|2002

DESIGN
Ottenwälder und
Ottenwälder,
Schwäbisch Gmünd

TITLE
CeBIT 2004

TYPE OF WORK
Outdoor advertising
campaign, posters

CLIENT
Konica Minolta
Business Solutions
Europe GmbH,
Langenhagen

APPEARED IN
03|2004

DESIGN
KP&Z Werbeagentur
GmbH, Münster
Martin Potrafke,
Nils Kölker,
Albrecht Hauss,
Marcus Podorf

TITLE
Pocketchu!

TYPE OF WORK
Cell phone information service

CLIENT
Chubu Electric Power Co., Inc., Nagoya seneca, Nagoya

APPEARED IN
02|2004

DESIGN
CID Lab., Shinnoske Inc., Osaka Yukichi Takada, Shinnoske Sugisaki, Chiaki Okuno

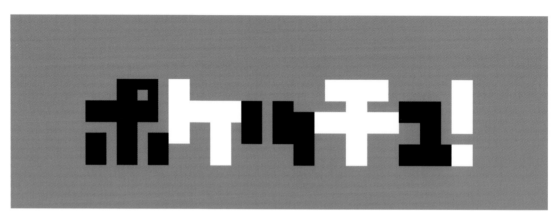

new@cep.jp

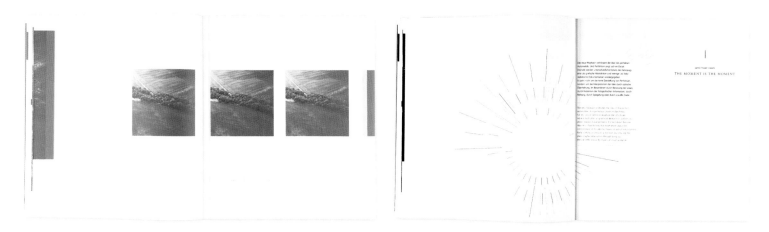

TITLE
Maybach/timeless

TYPE OF WORK
Brochure

CLIENT
DaimlerChrysler AG
Maybach Sales &
Marketing

APPEARED IN
05|2003

DESIGN
Bruce B. GmbH,
Stuttgart
recom GmbH,
Ostfildern
Creative direction:
Thomas Fritz,
Thomas Elser,
Thomas Waschke
Art direction:
Thomas Waschke
Photography:
Markus Bolsinger
Artworker:
Grit Hackenberg,
Thomas Saalfrank,
Thomas Fritz,
Marion Zeh

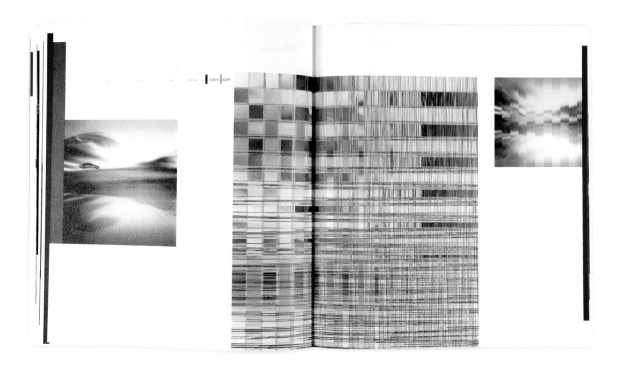

part 3 | the Archive of Change
THE FUTURE IS THE PAST

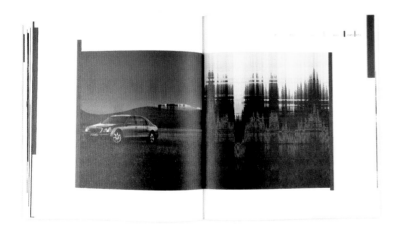

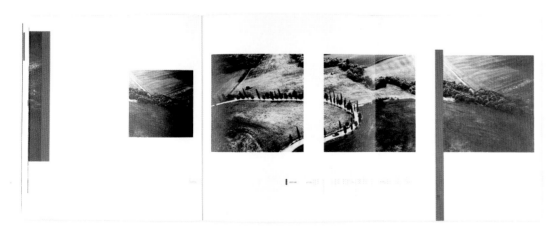

TITLE
Outtakes

TYPE OF WORK
Cinema spot

CLIENT
McDonald's Deutsch-
land Inc., Munich

APPEARED IN
10|2003

DESIGN
Heye & Partner
GmbH, Unterhaching
Thorsten Meier,
Norbert Herold,
Claudia Siegert
Director:
Andreas Hoffmann
TV production:
Big Fish

TITLE
Handtuch

TYPE OF WORK
Cinema spot

CLIENT
Orion Versand GmbH
& Co. KG, Flensburg

APPEARED IN
04|2004

DESIGN
Heye & Partner
GmbH, Unterhaching
Martin Goyne,
Nicole Oberberger,
Florian Ege
Director:
Ernst Kalff
TV production:
R.E.M.

137

TITLE
Keine Gegenfrage

TYPE OF WORK
TV spots

CLIENT
McDonald's Deutsch-
land Inc., Munich

APPEARED IN
01|2004

DESIGN
Heye & Partner
GmbH, Unterhaching
Thomas Winklbauer,
Florian Ege
Director:
Frieder Wittich
TV production:
Embassy of Dreams

TITLE
Architektur der
Obdachlosigkeit

TYPE OF WORK
Integrated campaign

CLIENT
BISS e.V., Munich

DESIGN
Heye & Partner GmbH,
Unterhaching
Ralph Taubenberger,
Joerg Jahn,
Marie-Luise Dorst,
José de Almeida,
Sabine Moll,
Päivi Helander,
Georg Rudolph,
Jan Weiler,
Dr. Karin Sagner

TITLE
Halbe Miete
(junior award)

TYPE OF WORK
Advertising campaign
for a magazine for
the homeless

CLIENT
fiftyfifty, Düsseldorf

APPEARED IN
12|2003

DESIGN
Felix Hornung,
Cologne

eine kampagne gegen obdachlosigkeit, entwickelt von felix hornung am fachbereich design der fachhochschule düsseldorf, gefördert von sappi : ideas that matter   www.fiftyfifty-galerie.de

eine kampagne gegen obdachlosigkeit, entwickelt von felix hornung am fachbereich design der fachhochschule düsseldorf, gefördert von sappi : ideas that matter   www.fiftyfifty-galerie.de

eine kampagne gegen obdachlosigkeit, entwickelt von felix hornung am fachbereich design der fachhochschule düsseldorf, gefördert von sappi : ideas that matter   www.fiftyfifty-galerie.de

WILDWECHSEL. EIN EINZELNES SCHABEN-WEIBCHEN KANN IN ANDERTHALB JAHREN IHRE WOHNUNG BIS ZUR DECKE MIT NACHKOMMEN FÜLLEN. BISSCHEN VIEL ARBEIT FÜR IHR BEIL. SEIEN SIE EIN SCHLECHTER GASTGEBER – **RUFEN SIE UNS AN.**

VERBAND DEUTSCHER SCHÄDLINGSBEKÄMPFER

FON 0800.819 81 31

TITLE
Kommunikations-konzept für Kammer-jäger
(junior award)

TYPE OF WORK
Undergraduate dissertation

CLIENT
Bergische Universität Wuppertal
Prof. Hans Günter Schmitz,
Prof. Dr. Dr. h.c. Siegfried Maser
(supervising professors)

APPEARED IN
03|2004

DESIGN
Daniela Höhmann, Wuppertal

JAGDZEIT. MÄUSE SIND FRÜHREIF. DAS MACHT SCHNELL AUS ZWEI MÄUSEN ZWEI-TAUSEND. MIT IHRER VASE KOMMEN SIE DA NICHT WEIT. SEIEN SIE EIN SCHLECHTER GASTGEBER – **RUFEN SIE UNS AN.**

VERBAND DEUTSCHER SCHÄDLINGSBEKÄMPFER

FON 0800.819 81 31

HAUSPUTZ. ALLES WAS SILBERFISCHE AM LEBEN HÄLT, FINDET SICH AUCH BEI IHNEN ZU HAUS. TAPETEN, BÜCHER, TEXTILIEN, FOTOS, ZUCKER, HAARE. MIT DEM HAMMER JAGEN SIE DEN TIEREN KEINE ANGST EIN. SEIEN SIE EIN SCHLECHTER GASTGEBER – **RUFEN SIE UNS AN.**

VERBAND DEUTSCHER SCHÄDLINGSBEKÄMPFER

FON 0800.819 81 31

TITLE
Chair Play

TYPE OF WORK
Advertising campaign

CLIENT
Interstuhl Büromöbel
GmbH & Co.KG,
Meßstetten-Tieringen

APPEARED IN
04|2004

DESIGN
ca concepts,
Scheuring
Christian Aichner
janacernodesign,
Munich
Jana Cerno

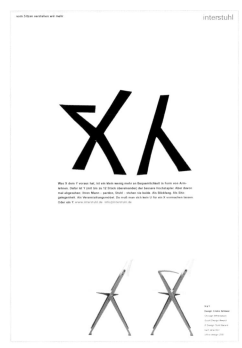

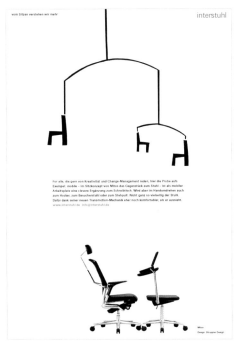

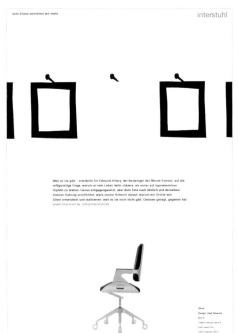

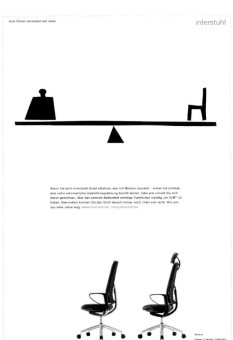

Hü, sagt der Intendant, Hott, der Veranstalter. Wo drei Menschen zusammensitzen, gibt es ein Dutzend Meinungen. Darum bieten wir für solche Anlässe mehr als eine Lösung – und auch mehr als die vier, die Sie hier sehen. Converso, X & Y, Ritmo oder IXC Berlin? Hü oder Hott? Diskutieren Sie erstmal. Was immer dabei rauskommt – bereuen werden Sie Ihre Entscheidung nicht. Da geben wir Ihnen unser Hü drauf. Und warten gespannt auf Ihr Hott: www.interstuhl.de info@interstuhl.de

von links nach rechts:
Converso
Design: Claudio Bellini,
Ritmo
Design: Puchta & Hagge,
X & Y
Design: Emilio Ambasz,
IXC Berlin
Design: gewerk

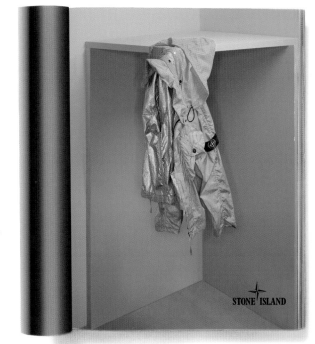

TITLE
Stone Island SS04

TYPE OF WORK
Advertising campaign,
catalogue

CLIENT
Sportswear Company,
Ravarino

APPEARED IN
03|2004

DESIGN
Agentur-E, Berlin
Marcus Gaab,
Christiane Bördner

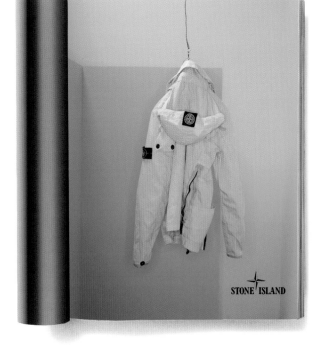

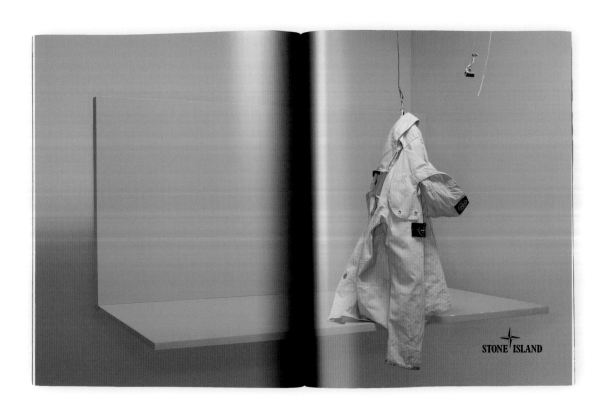

144

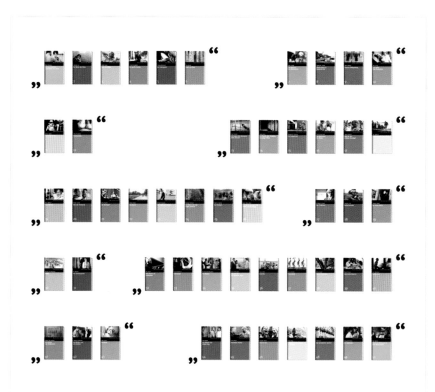

Verwirrt? Macht nichts. Canetti hat in Marrakesch auch nicht alles verstanden.

Ab morgen im Handel: Elias Canettis atmosphärischer Reisebericht „Die Stimmen von Marrakesch". Einer von 50 großen Romanen des 20. Jahrhunderts. Ausgewählt von der Feuilletonredaktion der Süddeutschen Zeitung. Liebevoll gestaltet und dabei besonders günstig. Jeden Samstag erscheint ein neuer Band als Hardcover mit Schutzumschlag. Erhältlich im Buchhandel, an ausgewählten Verkaufsstellen der Süddeutschen Zeitung und unter www.sz-bibliothek.de.

Lese. Freude. Sammeln.   Süddeutsche Zeitung | Bibliothek

TITLE
Die Anzeigenkam-
pagne SZ-Bibliothek

TYPE OF WORK
1/1 advertisement

CLIENT
Süddeutsche Zeitung
GmbH, Munich

APPEARED IN
04|2004–06|2004

DESIGN
GBK, Heye Werbe-
agentur GmbH,
Munich

Statt aus Glas haben wir „Stadt aus Glas"
von Paul Auster aus Büchern gebaut.

Nach Band 1 und Band 2 kommt jetzt
völlig überraschend: Band 3.

Band 5 ist da! Musikalisch mindestens so wichtig
wie Band 1, 2, 3 und 4 zusammen.

Rahmen nicht im Lieferumfang enthalten.

Anstoß Kundera, der gibt ab zu Umberto Eco
auf die andere Seite, Grass steht frei, spielt
Katz und Maus mit dem Gegner, weiter zu
Fitzgerald, in großen Sätzen rüber auf Thomas
Bernhard. Da schnappt sich Auster den Ball,
flankt zu Canetti, Canetti zu Forster. Walser
kommt ins Spiel, gibt blitzschnell ab zu John
Irving. Der interpretiert die Situation richtig,
spielt auf Onetti im Sechzehnmeterraum. Jetzt
darf er sich keinen Schnitzler erlauben... Foul,
böses Foul. Ganz klarer Elfmeter. Und wir sehen
Angst in den Augen des Tormanns. Handke mit
der Nr. 13. Was für eine Spannung, das dürfen
Sie sich nicht entgehen lassen.

TITLE
Persil "Farbpalette"

TYPE OF WORK
Advertisement

CLIENT
Henkel Wasch- und
Reinigungsmittel
GmbH, Düsseldorf

APPEARED IN
05|2004

DESIGN
BBDO Campaign
GmbH, Düsseldorf
Art director:
Alexander Spang
Creative director:
Veikko Hille
Copywriter:
Isabel Wischermann

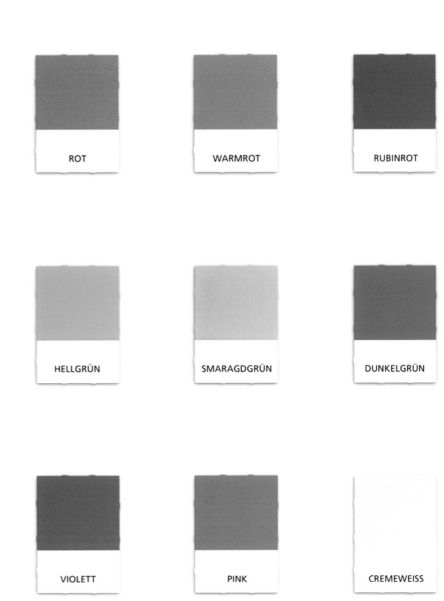

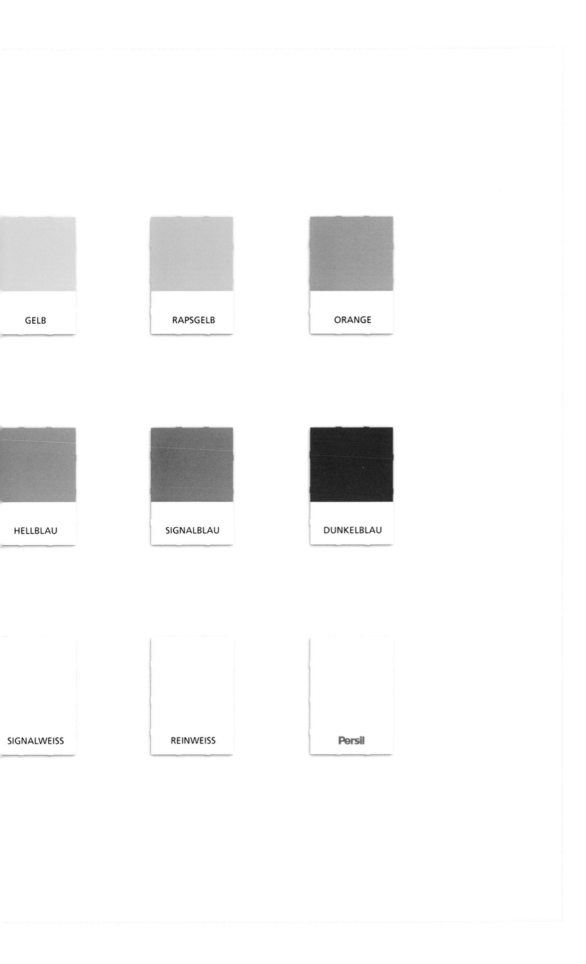

GELB

RAPSGELB

ORANGE

HELLBLAU

SIGNALBLAU

DUNKELBLAU

SIGNALWEISS

REINWEISS

Persil

TITLE
New March

TYPE OF WORK
Advertising campaign

CLIENT
Nissan Motor Co., Ltd.,
Tokyo

APPEARED IN
03|2002

DESIGN
Hakuhodo in progress
inc., Tokyo

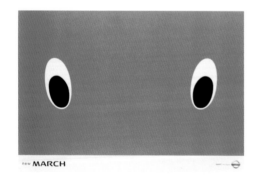

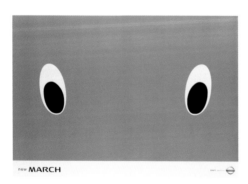

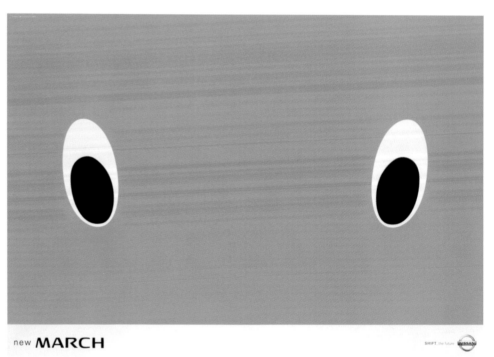

new color!

mango orange!

new **MARCH**

SHIFT_the future

RED DOT UNTERNEHMENSKOMMUNIKATION
Erscheinungsbilder | Logos | Geschäftsausstattung | CD-Manuals
Agenturselbstdarstellungen | Firmendarstellungen | Sonstiges

Jury:
Mervyn Kurlansky
Guy Schockaert
Kurt Weidemann

RED DOT CORPORATE COMMUNICATION
Corporate Image | Logos | Business Materials | CD Manuals
Self-Presentations by Agencies | Corporate Presentations | Others

TITLE
Versus FTS_VS_PIX

TYPE OF WORK
Book

APPEARED IN
03|2004

DESIGN
Magma [Büro für
Gestaltung], Karlsruhe
Axel Brinkmann,
Christian Ernst,
Lars Harmsen,
Boris Kahl,
Chris Steurer,
Ulrich Weiß

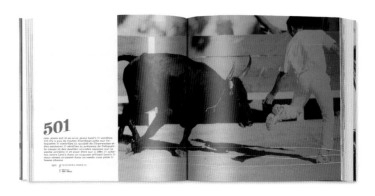

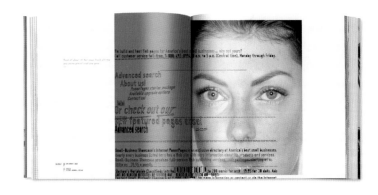

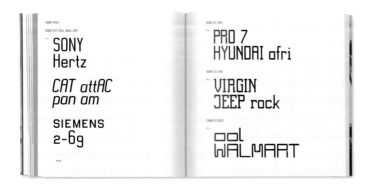

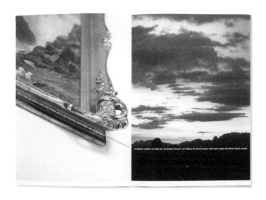

TITLE
die designgruppe
koop[3]

TYPE OF WORK
Self-presentation,
brochure

DESIGN
designgruppe koop[3],
Nesselwang

153

TYPE OF WORK
Corporate design

CLIENT
Fa. realize99, Graz

APPEARED IN
06|2003

DESIGN
alexgrimm,
Graz

TITLE
Leuchtensystem
Occhio von
Axelmeiselicht

TYPE OF WORK
Repositioning of the
Occhio brand

CLIENT
AML Licht + Design,
Munich

APPEARED IN
2003–2004

DESIGN
Martin et Karczinski,
Munich
Peter Martin,
Birgit Fuhrmeister,
Daniel Karczinski

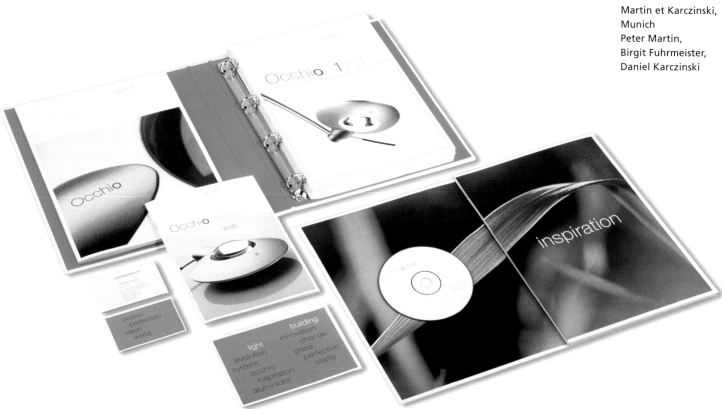

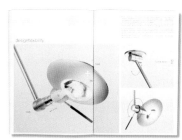

TITLE
Weg Zeichen /
My type of place

TYPE OF WORK
Book

APPEARED IN
12|2003

DESIGN
Andreas Uebele,
büro uebele
visuelle kommuni-
kation, Stuttgart

TITLE
Imagebroschüre

TYPE OF WORK
Corporate presentation

CLIENT
Buchbinderei Raymund
Henrich, Weißenfeld

APPEARED IN
01|2004

DESIGN
Fa-Ro Marketing GmbH,
Munich
Sabrina Ruchti,
Thomas Mayer

TITLE
Transsolar Klima-
Engineering

TYPE OF WORK
Book

CLIENT
Transsolar Energie-
technik, Stuttgart

APPEARED IN
11|2003

DESIGN
büro uebele visuelle
kommunikation,
Stuttgart
Katrin Häfner,
Margarethe Saxler,
Andreas Uebele,
Christine Voshage

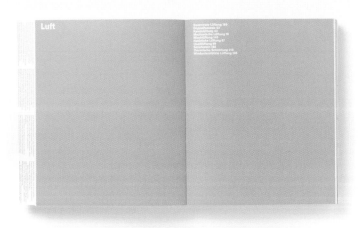

Im Hinblick auf unsere Entwicklungs-
geschichte gehört das Heim zum
Menschsein. Als Höhlenmenschen
bezeichnen wir die frühesten Ver-
treter unserer Art. Der Mensch sucht
sich sein Haus, der Mensch macht
sich sein Heim – und wird gerade
dadurch zum Menschen.

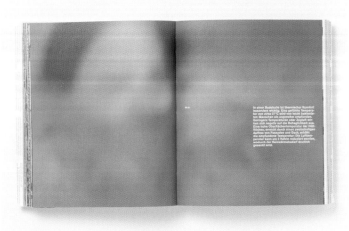

Wie lässt sich Licht bestmöglich
nutzen?

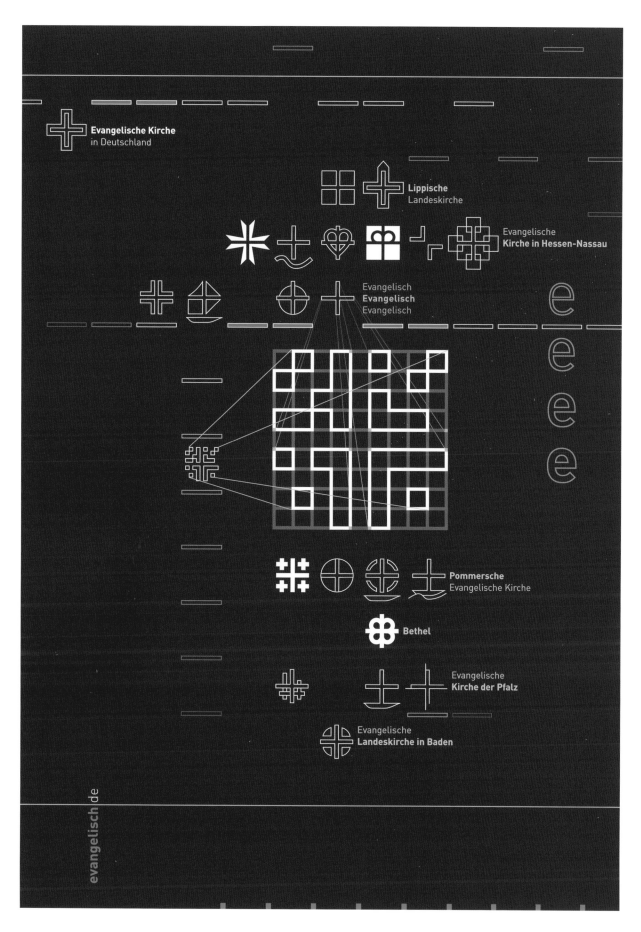

Evangelische Kirche
in Deutschland

Lippische
Landeskirche

Evangelische
Kirche in Hessen-Nassau

Evangelisch
Evangelisch
Evangelisch

Pommersche
Evangelische Kirche

Bethel

Evangelische
Kirche der Pfalz

Evangelische
Landeskirche in Baden

evangelisch.de

TITLE
EKD, Evangelische
Kirche in Deutschland
(junior award)

TYPE OF WORK
Corporate identity

APPEARED IN
2003

DESIGN
Takeshi Otani, Berlin

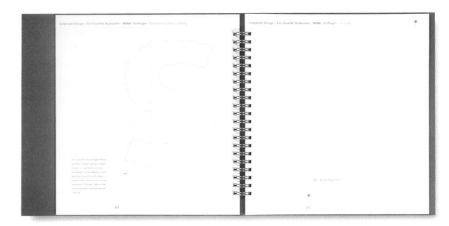

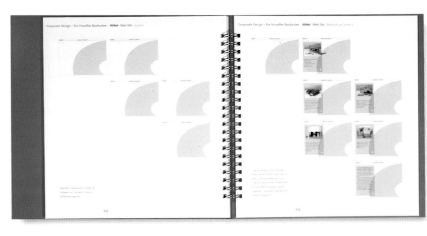

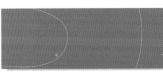

TITLE
Corporate Design für
(m)ein Designbüro
(junior award)

TYPE OF WORK
Corporate
communication

APPEARED IN
03|2004

DESIGN
Simone Hark-Schmidt,
Offenbach am Main

TITLE
Staves

TYPE OF WORK
Wine labels and
packaging

CLIENT
Tenuta Kornell-Staves,
Siebeneich (Bozen)

APPEARED IN
02|2004

DESIGN
Heye & Partner GmbH,
Unterhaching
Florian Drahorad,
Dominik Neubauer

TITLE
Issue 2003

TYPE OF WORK
Self-presentation

APPEARED IN
09|2003

DESIGN
Gingco Werbeagentur
GmbH & Co. KG,
Braunschweig
Jörg-Uwe Argo,
Martin Bretschneider

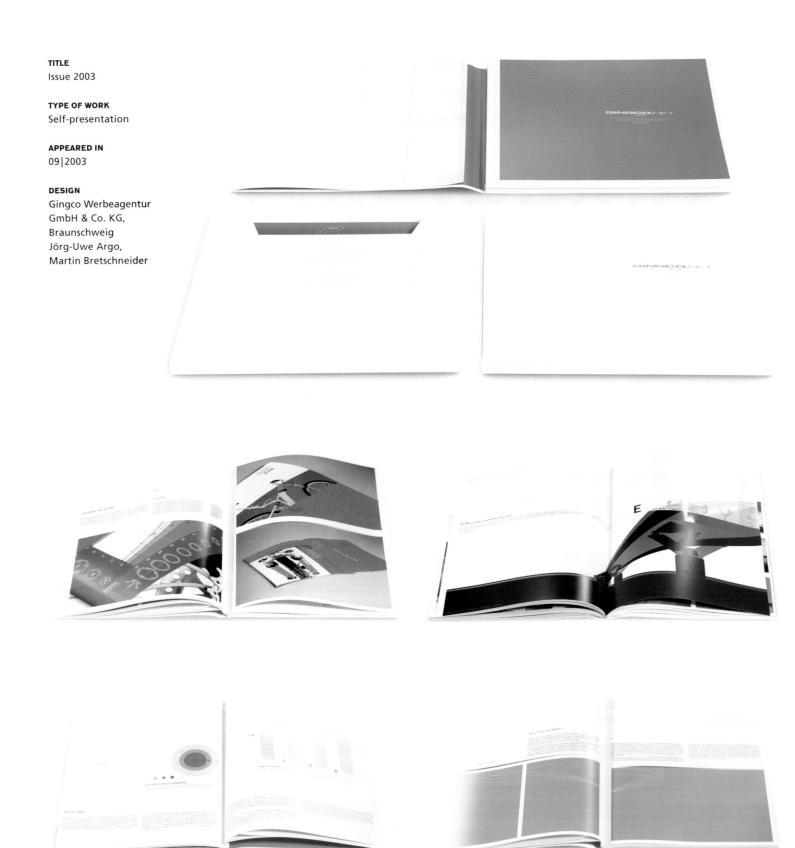

TITLE
Corporate Identity.
Kleiner Leitfaden und
neun kurze
Geschichten

TYPE OF WORK
CD manual for O_2
staff

CLIENT
O_2 (Germany) GmbH
& Co. OHG, Munich

APPEARED IN
05|2003

DESIGN
KMS Team GmbH,
Munich
Creative direction:
Michael Keller
Art direction:
Thorsten Buch,
Julia Just
Copy: Axel Sanjosé
Voice: Nicolas Böll
Project management:
Lioba Scherzer

TITLE
KMS Lach- und
Sachgeschichten

TYPE OF WORK
Self-presentation,
Christmas mailing

APPEARED IN
12|2003

DESIGN
KMS Team GmbH,
Munich
Creative direction:
Michael Keller,
Knut Maierhofer,
Christoph Rohrer
Concept:
Knut Maierhofer
Direction, camera,
editing: Dirk Koy,
Cecil Rustemeyer
Script:
Christoph Rohrer
Voice:
Knut Maierhofer

TITLE
Corporate design &
corporate identity
lichtpunkt//netzwerk
für gestaltung
(junior award)

TYPE OF WORK
Undergraduate
dissertation

CLIENT
Schule für Gestaltung,
Ravensburg

APPEARED IN
07|2003

DESIGN
engenhart visuelle
kommunikation,
Winnenden
Marc Engenhart
nico hensel gestaltung,
Heidenheim
Nico Hensel

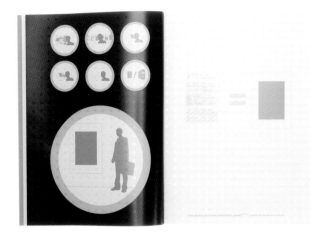

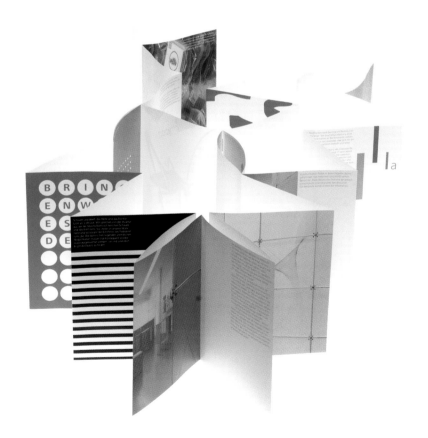

TITLE
Stiftung Saarlän-
discher Kulturbesitz

TYPE OF WORK
Corporate image

CLIENT
Stiftung Saarlän-
discher Kulturbesitz,
Saarbrücken

DESIGN
KMS Team GmbH,
Munich
Creative direction:
Michael Keller
Art direction:
Julia Just,
Peta Kobrow
Project management:
Lioba Scherzer

DER TAG, AN DEM
ABENDS DIE SONNE
AUFGEHT.

DER PLATZ GEHÖRT DIR.

THIS SEAT IS FOR YOU!

DER PLATZ
GEHÖRT DIR.

KATEGORIEN   CATEGORIES

WETTBEWERBSUNTERLAGEN   CONDITIONS OF PARTICIPATION

DIE NACHT
GEHÖRT DIR.

TITLE
VDW Award 04

TYPE OF WORK
Presentation of an
advertising film
award

CLIENT
VdW Verband
deutscher Werbefilm-
produzenten e.V.,
Hamburg

APPEARED IN
04|2004

DESIGN
Group.IE GmbH,
Frankfurt / Main
Kai Bergmann

WEGGEGANGEN,
PLATZ VERGANGEN.

RESERVIERT FÜR

TUMMELPLATZ
DER GEFÜHLE.

BESESSEN
SEIT 1966.

DER KOPF
SITZT OBEN.

SITZFLEISCH
DE LUXE.

WENN DIE GANZE
WELT EINE BÜHNE
IST, WO SITZEN DANN
DIE ZUSCHAUER?

DER TAG, AN DEM
ABENDS DIE SONNE
AUFGEHT.

TITLE
Team Friedensallee 120

TYPE OF WORK
Corporate presentation

CLIENT
Langebartels & Jürgens
Druckerei GmbH,
Hamburg

APPEARED IN
07|2004

DESIGN
Format Design,
Hamburg
Knut Ettling

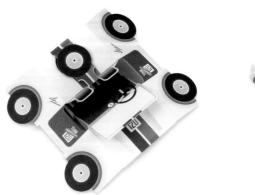

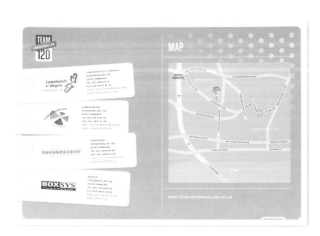

TITLE
Open Systems AG

TYPE OF WORK
Corporate
presentation

CLIENT
Open Systems AG,
Zurich

APPEARED IN
10|2003

DESIGN
Büro4
Gestaltung und
Kommunikation,
Zurich
Photography:
Noë Flum, Zurich

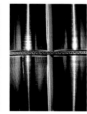

TITLE
Etwas Passendes

TYPE OF WORK
Self-presentation

APPEARED IN
07 | 2002

DESIGN
Art+Work=
Werbeagentur,
Frankfurt / Main
Creative direction:
Dieter Hopf
Art direction:
Almut Riebe
Photography:
Alex Schwander

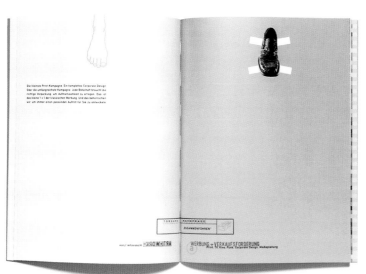

TITLE
Neuheiten Broschüre
04

TYPE OF WORK
Brochure

CLIENT
COR Sitzmöbel,
Rheda-Wiedenbrück

APPEARED IN
01/2004

DESIGN
Factor Design AG,
Hamburg
Verena Baumhögger,
Olaf Stein

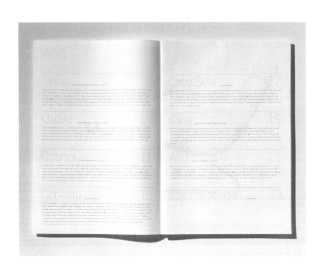

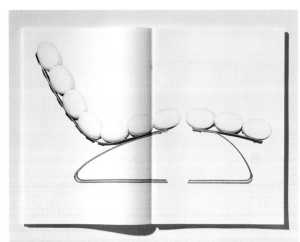

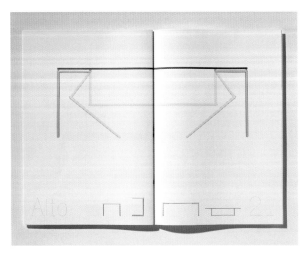

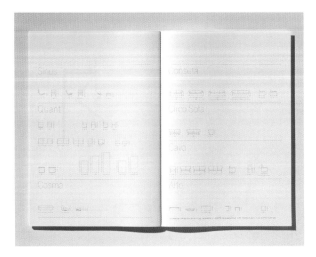

TITLE
COR Jubiläumsbuch

TYPE OF WORK
Book

CLIENT
COR Sitzmöbel,
Rheda-Wiedenbrück

APPEARED IN
01/2004

DESIGN
Factor Design AG,
Hamburg
Jan Kruse,
Olaf Stein,
Sonja Stroth,
Verena Baumhögger,
Lin Lambert

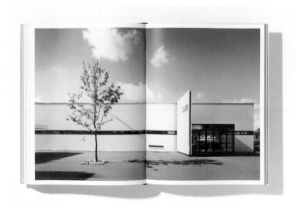

TITLE
10Y FD

TYPE OF WORK
Self-presentation

APPEARED IN
01/2004

DESIGN
Factor Design AG,
Hamburg
Johannes Erler,
Christian Tönsmann

TITLE
SintLucas

TYPE OF WORK
Corporate identity

CLIENT
SintLucas (School for
Communication and
Design), Boxtel

APPEARED IN
2003

DESIGN
Concept and design:
Eric Hesen, Amsterdam
Erik Kessels, Amsterdam
Copywriter:
Franklin Neutenboom,
Utrecht

TITLE
Dubrovnik Museums

TYPE OF WORK
Corporate identity,
individual logos

CLIENT
Dubrovnik Museums,
Dubrovnik

APPEARED IN
05|2003

DESIGN
Laboratorium,
Zagreb
Orsat Franković,
Ivana Vučić

DU'M | DUBROVAČKI MUZEJI
DUBROVNIK MUSEUMS

KNEŽEV DVOR / RECTOR'S PALACE
Kulturno - povijesni muzej
Cultural - Historical museum

RUPE
Etnografski muzej
Etnographical Museum

Pomorski muzej
Maritime Museum

Muzej suvremene povijesti
Contemporary History Museum

Arheološki muzej
Archeological Museum

Dom Marina Držića
House of Marin Držić

TITLE
BELUX AG

TYPE OF WORK
Poster

CLIENT
BELUX AG, Birsfelden

DESIGN
Design 3
Jolanda Luethy,
Baden

Protestantse Kerk

TITLE
De Protestantse Kerk
in Nederland

TYPE OF WORK
Corporate identity

CLIENT
Dienstenorganisatie
Protestantse Kerk,
Utrecht

APPEARED IN
05|2004

DESIGN
Total Identity BV,
Amsterdam
Aad van Dommelen,
André Mol,
Guido van Breda

TITLE
Erscheinungsbild
Martin et Karczinski

TYPE OF WORK
Business materials,
case studies

APPEARED IN
01|2002

DESIGN
Martin et Karczinski,
Munich
Peter Martin,
Daniel Karczinski,
Nicola Sacher,
Birgit Fuhrmeister,
Antje Stumpe

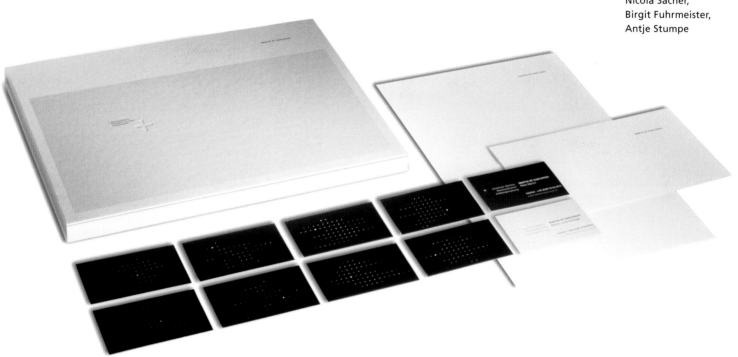

TITLE
Siemens Mobile
Corporate Identity/
Corporate Design

TYPE OF WORK
Corporate
communication

CLIENT
Siemens AG, Munich

APPEARED IN
04|2004

DESIGN
METADESIGN AG,
Berlin
Heike Albig,
Daniel Thoma,
Luca Iaconelli,
André Metzen

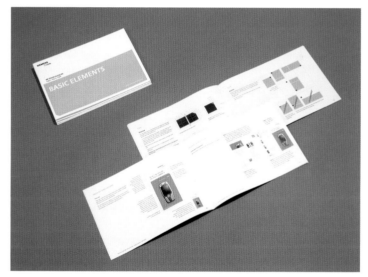

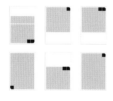

SIEMENS MOBILE
HEADLINE WITH
THREE LINES

15 pt
24 pt
39 pt   *
63 pt

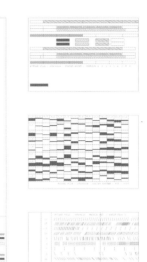

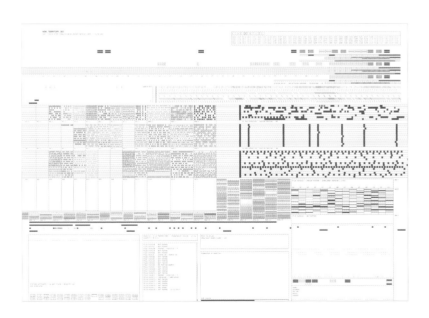

TITLE
Solar Initiative

TYPE OF WORK
Corporate identity
and self-presentation

DESIGN
Solar Initiative,
Amsterdam
Miguel Gori,
Ivo Schmetz

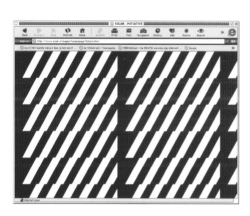

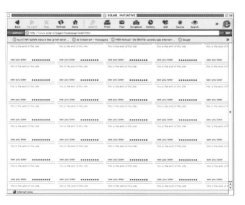

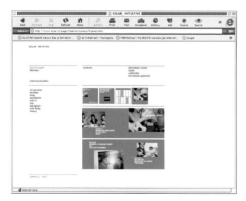

TITLE
Porsche Lizenz- und
Handelsgesellschaft

TYPE OF WORK
Corporate design

CLIENT
Porsche Lizenz- und
Handelsgesellschaft
mbH & Co. KG,
Bietigheim-Bissingen

APPEARED IN
07|2004

DESIGN
KMS Team GmbH,
Munich
Creative direction:
Knut Maierhofer
Design team:
Patrick Märki,
Dirk Koy
Project management:
Sandra Ehm
Production super-
vision:
Christina Baur

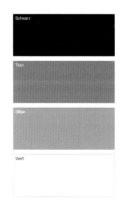

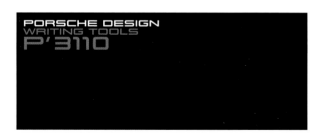

184

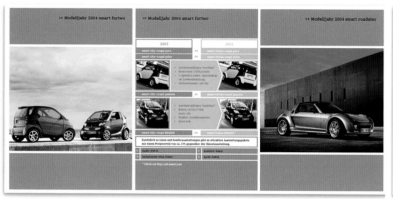
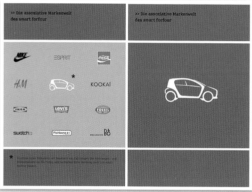

TITLE
smart forfour
Eurotraining 2004

TYPE OF WORK
Communication media
for participants

CLIENT
DaimlerChrysler AG,
Stuttgart

APPEARED IN
03|2004

DESIGN
büro diffus GmbH,
Stuttgart

TITLE
In 80 Days Around
The World

TYPE OF WORK
Image campaign,
corporate presentation

CLIENT
Würth Medien GmbH,
Rudersberg

APPEARED IN
02|2004

DESIGN
Communication:
aexea Integrierte
Kommunikation,
Stuttgart
Conception:
yama inc. – Büro für
Gestaltung, Stuttgart
Photography:
Yvonne Seidel,
Stuttgart

TITLE
Corporate identity

TYPE OF WORK
Corporate identity

CLIENT
Nationaal Archief,
Den Haag

APPEARED IN
2002–2003

DESIGN
UNA (Amsterdam)
designers,
Amsterdam

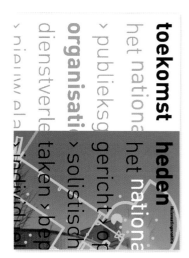

187

RED DOT FINANZKOMMUNIKATION
Imagebroschüren | Geschäftsberichte | Haus- und Mitarbeiterzeitschriften | Sonstiges

RED DOT FINANCIAL COMMUNICATION
Image Brochures | Annual Reports | House and Staff Magazines | Others

Jury:
Mervyn Kurlansky
Guy Schockaert
Kurt Weidemann

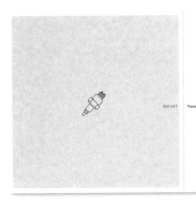

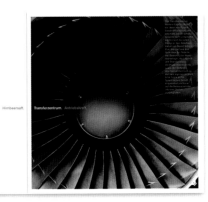

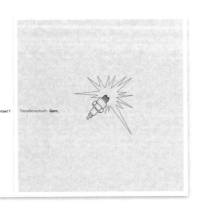

TITLE
Bosch Transferzentrum
Venture Capital

TYPE OF WORK
Image brochure

CLIENT
Bosch Transferzentrum
Venture Capital,
Stuttgart

APPEARED IN
10|2003

DESIGN
Beaufort 8 GmbH,
Stuttgart
Christine Elsässer,
Annette Petry,
Sabine Schmidt,
Philipp Heimsch

TITLE
Trust – Business on a
Different Level

TYPE OF WORK
Image brochure

CLIENT
Siemens Business
Services, Munich

APPEARED IN
03|2004

DESIGN
Beierarbeit, Bielefeld

TITLE
akf bank Geschäfts-
bericht 2002/2003

TYPE OF WORK
Annual report

CLIENT
akf bank, Wuppertal
Petra Hattab
Büro für Design,
Düsseldorf

APPEARED IN
01|2004

DESIGN
herzogenrathsaxler
kommunikationsdesign,
Düsseldorf
Matthias Herzogenrath,
Margarethe Saxler

TITLE
We will.

TYPE OF WORK
Annual report

CLIENT
adidas-Salomon AG,
Herzogenaurach

APPEARED IN
03|2004

DESIGN
häfelinger + wagner
design, Munich
Frank Wagner,
Kerstin Weidemeyer,
Katharina von Hellberg

Gerannt. Geackert. Geschrien.

Gerannt. Geackert. Geschrien. Gejubelt. Geflucht. Gekracht. Umarmt. Vor Freude. Vor Glück. Denn wir sind am Ziel. Haben geschafft, was immer nur eine Mannschaft schaffen kann: Die Weltmeisterschaft. /// Deutsche Damen-Fußballnationalmannschaft / Weltmeister 2003.

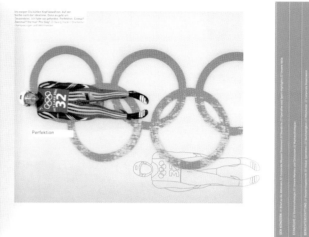

Im ewigen Eis kühlen Kopf bewahren. Auf der Suche nach der idealen Linie. Denn es geht um Zehntelsekunden. Ich habe sie gefunden. Perfektion. Energie? Skeleton? Warmup! Pro Sleep! /// Georg Hackl / Die feinen Unterscheidungen und Verfeinerungen

Perfektion

Herz und Verstand

Um so gewinnen braucht es mehr als nur den Fuß. Den Kopf und Verstand hat zu jeder Chance. /// Zinédine Zidane /// ...

adidas Sport Performance

Diese Division umfasst bahnbrechende Technologien wie ClimaCool®, a³™, die Predator® Fußballschuhfamilie sowie das neue Ground Control System™, und unseren neuen JetConcept™ Ganzkörperanzug. Mit unseren Performance-orientierten Produkten wollen wir die Leistungsfähigkeit von Sportlern jeder Niveau erhöhen und ihren speziellen Bedürfnissen gerecht werden.

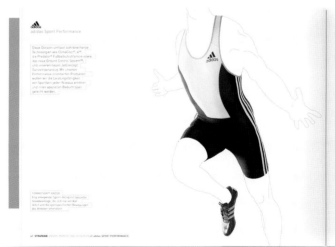

FORMOTION™ ANZUG
Eng anliegender Sport-Anzug mit speziellen Gewebezonen, die sich nie verkleben. Jetzt und bei geringen kleinen Bewegungen des Athleten unterstützen.

adiPure LIGHTSPRINT
Der Sportschuh mit extrem leichter Sohle bei seinen Spikes an die Füße des Läufers und der regelmäßiger Feldmesser.

195

TITLE
on·top*

TYPE OF WORK
E.ON annual report
2003

CLIENT
E.ON AG, Düsseldorf

APPEARED IN
04|2004

DESIGN
Lesmo, Düsseldorf

*Führung

*Führung

Der integrierte Energiekonzern wird von einer starken Führungs-
gesellschaft, dem Corporate Center, geleitet. Das Corporate Center
optimiert das Strom- und Gasgeschäft über die Märkte hinweg
und trifft Entscheidungen für die Zukunft des Gesamtunternehmens.
Klare und ambitionierte Ziele für den Konzern und die Market Units,
fokussiertes Wachstum und die Integration der einzelnen Gesell-
schaften stehen dabei im Mittelpunkt. Um das Corporate Center zu
stärken, haben wir neue Führungsfunktionen etabliert und sämtliche
Führungsprozesse optimiert.

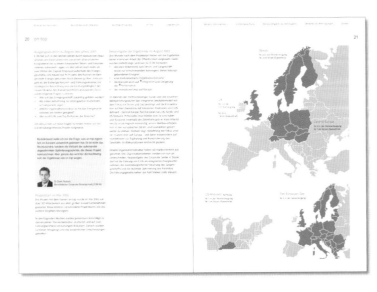

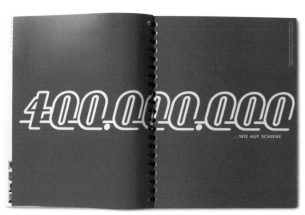

TITLE
ÖBB Planning and
Engineering

TYPE OF WORK
Image brochure

CLIENT
ÖBB – Austrian Railways, Infrastructure
Division

APPEARED IN
04|2004

DESIGN
Buero 16, Vienna
Peter Deisenberger,
Susanne Menger,
Barbara Theis

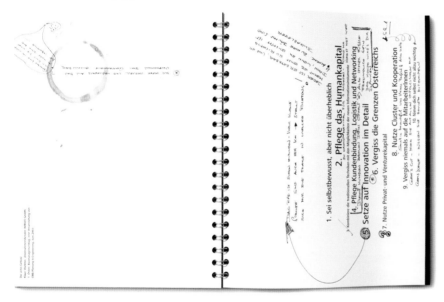

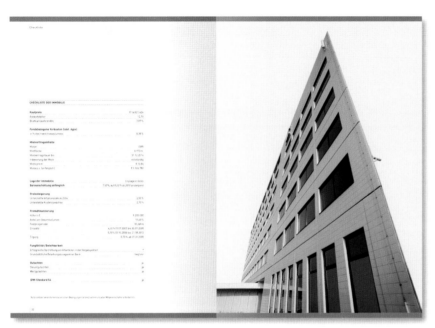

TITLE
Bankhaus Wölbern
Fondsprospekte

TYPE OF WORK
Pamphlets

CLIENT
Bankhaus Wölbern,
Hamburg

APPEARED IN
2002–2004

DESIGN
Incorporate, Berlin
Christine Meves

TITLE
HyundaiCard
Hyundai Capital

TYPE OF WORK
Annual report 2003

CLIENT
HyundaiCard Hyundai
Capital, Seoul

APPEARED IN
03|2004

DESIGN
S/O Project, Seoul
Hyun Cho,
Young-Sik Oh,
Dae-Ki Shim,
Hyun-Jae Lee,
Joong-Bae Kim

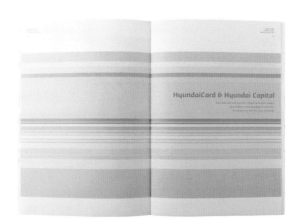
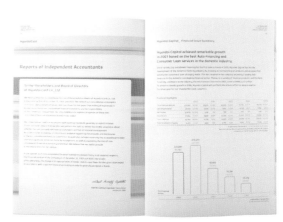

TITLE
Der eingebildete
Kranke
Annual 02

TYPE OF WORK
Pamphlet

CLIENT
Ogilvy & Mather
Deutschland,
Frankfurt/Main

APPEARED IN
05|2003

DESIGN
Tillmanns, Ogilvy &
Mather GmbH & Co. KG,
Düsseldorf
Jochen Smidt, Katja
Brunner, Simone Buch,
Frauke Berg

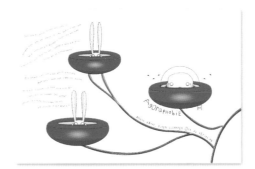

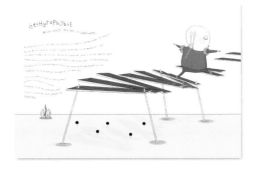

TITLE
ARTEEST

TYPE OF WORK
Staff magazine

CLIENT
E.ON Sales & Trading,
Munich

APPEARED IN
06|2003 – 04|2004

DESIGN
Lesmo, Düsseldorf

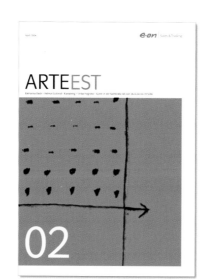

TITLE
Morgen

TYPE OF WORK
Annual report

CLIENT
Linde AG, Wiesbaden

APPEARED IN
03|2004

DESIGN
KW43
brandbuilding and
design, Düsseldorf

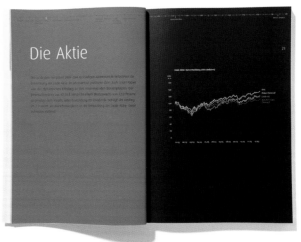

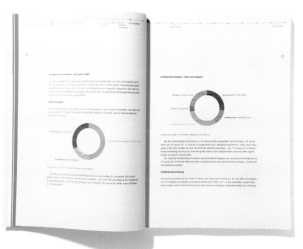

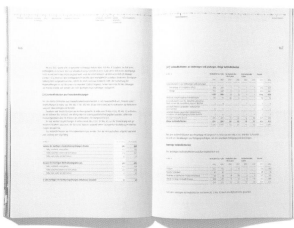

TITLE
Happy Birthday

TYPE OF WORK
Commemorative
book

CLIENT
JTC Corporation,
Singapore

APPEARED IN
19 November 2003

DESIGN
Epigram, Singapore
Zann Wan,
Yee-Ling Koh,
Roger Hiew

Shaping the Future
Daewoo Securities Annual Report FY2002

A continuous rebirth carries promises
That the cycle of life
In all of its subtle, blooming grace
Catches flight and finds its way

Your expectations are always met with us.

Contents

From the depths of the earth
To the transparency of water
Adaptable and growing with new possibilities
Of absolute contentedness.

Your life-long satisfaction is always our guarantee.

To Shareholders & Clients

>>> Dear Fellow Shareholders, Customers, and Investors

Fiscal year 2002 was a very challenging year for the Company. The wave of pride that swept the entire nation during the World Cup was interrupted as Korea came face-to-face with the reality of a faltering domestic and global economy. Events, such as the imminent threat of conflict in Iraq and concerns over North Korea's nuclear program, served to strip away the uncertainties surrounding the economy. Financial markets at home were also hit hard as the KOSPI, since considered a jewel of Asia's stock markets, continued to year-long slide that began in April of 2002.

As a result of such rapid changes and increased competition, the financial service industry has been forced to restructure itself according to market demands. Additionally, our existing business has reached their saturation points, as overheated competition finally took a toll on profitability. For the first time in Korean industry's history, one local securities firm voluntarily shuttered its operations. Not surprisingly, further trends toward financial integration are expected to intensify competition among players even more in the near future.

However, it is precisely during such uncertain times that threats like these can be turned into opportunities. In this manner, the year 2003 is expected to be a turnaround year for us as we work toward resolving difficulties and freeing ourselves from the burden of non-operating losses. Accordingly, Daewoo Securities endeavors to reset itself as one of the soundest and most transparent companies in the industry.

As a leading integrated financial service provider, Daewoo Securities has been laying the groundwork to become the best securities company in the Korean financial service industry. For this purpose, the Company has reorganized its business around the customer in order to respond more effectively to customer changing needs. We, at Daewoo Securities, will continue to make the future of the Korean financial service industry in this way.

Guided on a definitive path
As unburdened as the wind
New life is created and born
In nature's protective arms.

Your trust in us is always what we value most.

Management's Discussion & Analysis   15

>> Stock Market Performance

Fiscal year 2002 was a difficult year for financial markets all over the world. Concerns of a double dip in the U.S. economy, worries over North Korea's nuclear program, uncertainties about war in Iraq, problems with domestic credit card companies, and fears from the SARS epidemic further led to a decline in Korea's equity markets. The KOSPI, after soaring to a high of 943.95 points in April of 2002, dropped 43% by fiscal year-end to 535.70 points. Similarly, the technology-heavy KOSDAQ index, after peaking at 92.44 points in April of 2002, plunged 59% by fiscal year-end to 37.77 points.

Amid a sluggish equity market, equity trading value fell 15% in fiscal year 2002 to KRW 847 trillion, compared to KRW 1,000 trillion for the same period last year. Trading value in the Korea Stock Exchange (KSE) remained at similar levels seen last year at KRW 609 trillion, further supported by active arbitrage trading between equity and futures and the rising popularity of exchange traded funds (ETFs). The trading value in the KOSDAQ stock market, however, fell sharply by 40% from KRW 398 trillion last year to only KRW 238 trillion in fiscal year 2002.

Futures and options trading continued to rise, fueled by active trading by individual investors, whose trades accounted for 60% of total trading value. Trading value in the futures market grew 68% to KRW 2,193 trillion while trading in the options market increased 96% to KRW 136 trillion compared to the same period last year.

The benchmark 3-year Korean Treasury bond interest rate peaked at 6.47% in the first half of 2002 as economic indicators began to pick up on expectations of an early economic recovery. However, it ended the year at 4.78% as the government continued to maintain a low interest rate policy amid a prolonged slump in the real economy.

The beneficiary certificates market grew slightly until March of 2003 as it continued to attract investment funds. The total sales volume, however, dropped 10% due to measures restricting redemption after the SK Global scandal and ongoing problems of local credit card companies.

Underwriting volume dropped 20% to KRW 79 trillion compared to KRW 100 trillion in fiscal year 2001. Equity underwriting volume, including underwriting volume for IPOs, was especially hard hit as it fell by 52% to KRW 6 trillion primarily because of the slump in the KOSDAQ market.

TITLE
Daewoo Securities
2002 Annual Report

TYPE OF WORK
Annual report

CLIENT
Daewoo Securities Co.,
Ltd., Seoul

APPEARED IN
08|2002

DESIGN
Universal Corporate
Communications, Inc.,
Seoul
Mijung Lim

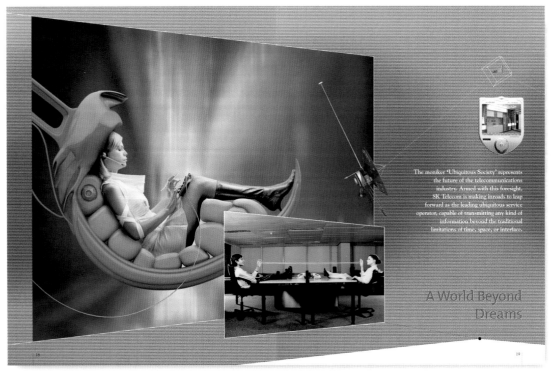

TITLE
SK Telecom 2003
Annual Report

TYPE OF WORK
Annual report

CLIENT
SK Telecom, Seoul

APPEARED IN
04|2003

DESIGN
Universal Corporate
Communications, Inc.,
Seoul
Mijung Lim

TITLE
Bon Appetit
(with distinction)

TYPE OF WORK
Annual report

CLIENT
Podravka d.d.,
Koprivnica

APPEARED IN
07|2003

DESIGN
Bruketa & Zinic,
Zagreb
Davor Bruketa,
Nikola Zinic

10 75

STUFFED ROAST MEAT IN WINE

75 dg rib roast or bones, stuffing: 2 pears, 5dg raisins without kernels, lemon juice, 12 dg one-day-old rolls, 2 tablespoons milk, 5dg butter, 1 egg, 1 yolk, parsley, salt, pepper, 4 tablespoons oil, 5 dg dried bacon, 1 onion bulb, 1 bundle soup vegetables (carrot, parsley, celery), 2 dl white wine, pepper grains, bay leaf, vinegar, 1 Vegeta tablespoon. First prepare the stuffing: cut pears and raisins (if necessary avoid them before) in cubes and sprinkle over with lemon juice. Cut rolls into cubes and sprinkle with 2 tablespoons of milk. Mix butter (3dg) fresnly with yolk and egg to combine and add bread and fruit cubes. Add salt, pepper, add freshly chopped parsley and mix well. Then prepare meat. Cut it into length and open like a book, so to get a big steak. Batter well, add pepper and sprinkle with Vegeta. Arrange the stuffing over the meat and roll firmly. Tie with thread and sprinkle with salt. Roast the meat all over in a hot sliced tin. Fry bacon, onions and vegetables separately in a pan and add to meat. Add a little vinegar and wine, add bay leaf and pepper grains. Cover with aluminum foil and bake in a pre-heated oven on 200°C for 60 minutes. Before baked remove the foil and brown, add the wine left and water if necessary. Remove from oven, remove thread and slice it. Arrange on a warm plate and baste with strainer run sauce mixed

FRIED CUTLETS WITH MUSHROOMS

8 small pork cutlets, salt, pepper, frying oil, 4dg butter, 20 dg mushrooms, 1 clove of garlic, parsley, 1 dl wine, 1 dl cream, 1 Vegeta teaspoon, hot pepper, Cut cutlets in ends, batter them. Sprinkle salt, pepper and fry on hot oil on both sides. Fry sliced mushrooms separately on hot butter. Add Vegeta, chopped garlic, hot pepper, add water and wine. Leave to boil shortly, add cream mixed with Gussnel. Baste fried hot cutlets with this sauce and sprinkle with chopped parsley. As trimming serve string noodles or potato croquettes.

RED DOT PRODUKTKOMMUNIKATION
Packungsdesign: Verkaufsverpackungen | Transportverpackungen | Displayverpackungen
Produktgrafik | Food-Design | Etiketten | Bedienungsanleitungen | Sonstiges

Jury:
Jean Jacques Schaffner
Frido Steinen-Broo
Stefan Ytterborn

RED DOT PRODUCT COMMUNICATION
Packaging Design: Sales Packaging | Transport Packaging | Display Packaging
Product Graphics | Food Design | Labels | Instructions | Others

TITLE
Karl Bartos
"Communication"

TYPE OF WORK
Packaging design

CLIENT
Home Records,
Hamburg
Sony Music, Berlin

APPEARED IN
09|2003

DESIGN
weissraum.de(sign),
Hamburg
Lucas Buchholz,
Bernd Brink

TITLE
Martini Frezzio

TYPE OF WORK
Packaging design

CLIENT
Bacardi España SA,
Mollet del Valles
Barcelona

APPEARED IN
09|2003

DESIGN
Ruiz + Company,
Torres & Torres,
Barcelona

TITLE
2 Take Away

TYPE OF WORK
Product
communication,
packaging design

CLIENT
Rösle GmbH & Co. KG,
Marktoberdorf

APPEARED IN
04|2004

DESIGN
loup.susanne wolf,
Stuttgart
Silke Braun,
Saskia Bannasch

TITLE
Intercontinental

TYPE OF WORK
Product
communication,
packaging design

CLIENT
Rösle GmbH & Co. KG,
Marktoberdorf

DESIGN
loup.susanne wolf,
Stuttgart
Silke Braun

TITLE
DTP Typometer

TYPE OF WORK
Typometer

CLIENT
Verlag Hermann
Schmidt Mainz, Mainz

DESIGN
strichpunkt, Stuttgart
Kirsten Dietz

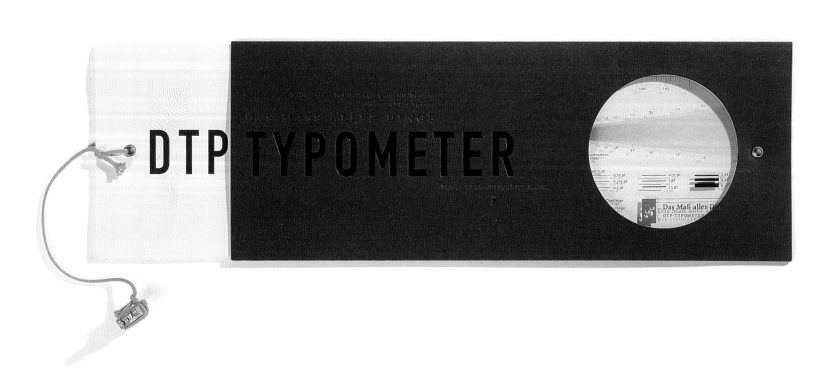

TITLE
Adventskalender
Ho Ho Ho

TYPE OF WORK
Advent calendar

APPEARED IN
11|2003

DESIGN
prime design
werbeagentur gmbh,
Hanover
Christoph Paul,
Thilo Uhlenkott

TITLE
Weinetiketten

TYPE OF WORK
Wine Labels

CLIENT
Michael Broger
Weinbau, Ottoberg

APPEARED IN
05|2004

DESIGN
Melanie Brunner,
Kreuzlingen
Alexandra Zemp,
Weinfelden

TITLE
La Femme Fenjal

TYPE OF WORK
Packaging design

CLIENT
Doetsch Grether AG,
Basle

DESIGN
Artefakt Industrie-
kultur, Darmstadt/
Jung von Matt

TITLE
Dado

TYPE OF WORK
Product
communication

CLIENT
Niepoort (Vinhos) S.A.,
Porto

APPEARED IN
2003

DESIGN
alessandri design,
Wien

TITLE
MC

TYPE OF WORK
Cigarette pack

CLIENT
TDR, Rovinj

APPEARED IN
11|2003

DESIGN
Bruketa & Zinic,
Zagreb
Miran Tomicic
Moe Minkara

TITLE
Quolofune

TYPE OF WORK
Packaging design

CLIENT
Quolofune, Osaka

APPEARED IN
10|2003

DESIGN
Shigeno Araki Design
Office, Osaka
Shigeno Araki

TITLE
Produkt-Salespräsenter

TYPE OF WORK
Product presenter

CLIENT
Joseph Chevalier
Montres SA, Le Sentier

DESIGN
Visualis GmbH,
Pforzheim
Helge Ulrich

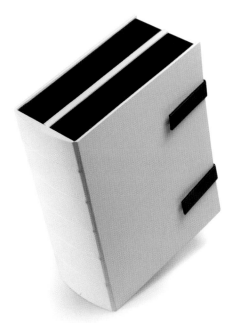

TITLE
FM radio clamshell

TYPE OF WORK
Packaging design

CLIENT
Nike Inc, Beaverton

APPEARED IN
2004

DESIGN
Nike Inc.
Creative direction/ID:
Ed Boyd,
Dave McLaughlin
Industrial design:
Josh Maruska,
Stefan Andren
Mechanical
engineering:
Samuel Huen,
Steve Berry
Art direction:
David Young
Graphic design:
Megan Chouinard
Photography:
Phillip Dixon

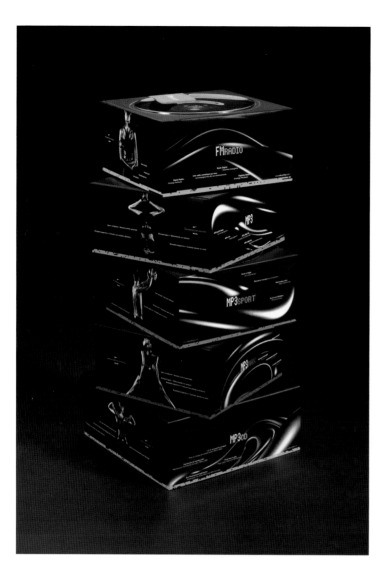

TITLE
MP3MAX BOX

TYPE OF WORK
Packaging design

CLIENT
Nike Inc, Beaverton

APPEARED IN
2004

DESIGN
Nike Inc.
Creative direction/ID:
Ed Boyd,
Dave McLaughlin
Industrial design:
Josh Maruska,
Stefan Andren
Mechanical
engineering:
Samuel Huen,
Steve Berry
Art direction:
David Young
Graphic design:
Megan Chouinard
Photography:
Phillip Dixon

In den sauren Apfel beißen – einmal kein Blatt vor den Mund nehmen. Die nackten Tatsachen auf den Tisch legen. Einfach mal dem Chef zeigen, wer die Socken anhat und Nein sagen! Nicht feige sein und Ja sagen zu der großen Liebe des Lebens. Also: Sich den Socken anziehen und Entscheidungen treffen.

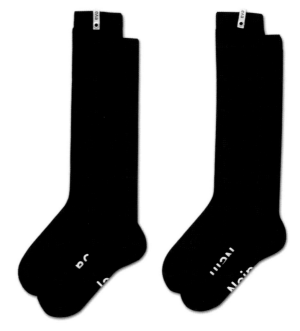

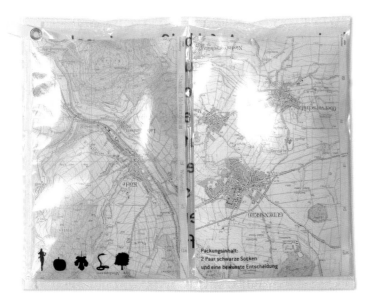

Packungsinhalt:
2 Paar schwarze Socken
und eine bewusste Entscheidung

Papier ist geduldig – Menschen weniger. Deshalb lieber mal kein Blatt vor den Mund nehmen und sich die Seele aus dem Leib schreiben. Andere nicht hinhalten. Entscheidungen treffen. Ja sagen oder Nein. Denn das Blatt kann sich auch wenden.

TITLE
eva. In den Apfel
beißen.
(junior award)

TYPE OF WORK
Product
communication,
undergraduate
dissertation

CLIENT
Fachhochschule
Darmstadt

APPEARED IN
01|2004

DESIGN
Eva Schubert, Bensheim
Eva Simonsen, Bensheim

Ein Leben wie im Paradies genießen – sich um nichts kümmern und ins gemachte Nest setzen. Das Paradies auf Erden? Nein! Schublade auf – den Stempel lasse ich mir nicht aufdrücken. Entscheidungen treffen ist nicht einfach. Doch nur so kommt man schon im Leben dem Paradies ein Stückchen näher.

Abwarten und Tee trinken? Entscheidungen, die nicht getroffen werden, sind auch welche. Aber will ich das wirklich? Keine trübe Tasse sein und nicht immer den kalten Kaffee von gestern schlürfen. Raus aus dem Alltagstrott! Das Leben auf der Zunge zergehen lassen.

Ich wasche meine Hände in Unschuld. Möchte kein Zankapfel sein, nichts ausbaden. Vornehme Rücksicht? Oder doch ins kalte Wasser springen? Wirklich sagen was man denkt: Ja! Oder Nein! Sich die Hände schmutzig machen und den Schweiß von der Stirn wischen.

RED DOT ÖFFENTLICHER RAUM
Messestände | Showrooms | Leit- und Orientierungssysteme | Elektronische Informationssysteme
Informationsdisplays | Ausstellungen | Signets und Piktogramme | Sonstiges

RED DOT PUBLIC AREAS
Trade Fair Stands | Showrooms | Signage and Guidance Systems | Electronic Information Systems
Information Displays | Exhibitions | Signets and Pictograms | Others

Jury:
Mervyn Kurlansky
Guy Schockaert
Kurt Weidemann

TITLE
Römische Badruinen
Baden-Baden

TYPE OF WORK
Public area

CLIENT
Staatliches Vermögens-
und Hochbauamt
Pforzheim

APPEARED IN
07|2003

DESIGN
büro uebele visuelle
kommunikation,
Stuttgart
Andreas Uebele,
Gerd Häussler

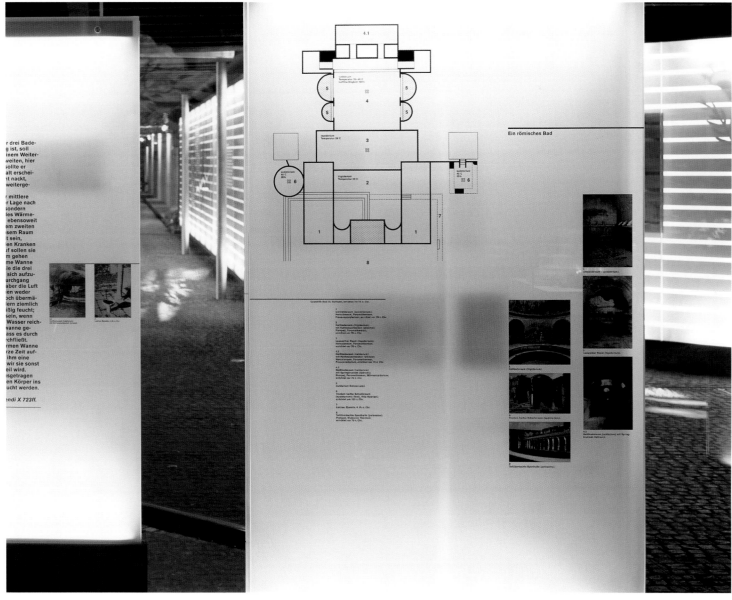

TITLE
LED environment for
historic computers

TYPE OF WORK
Installation for an
exhibition of the
Neue Sammlung
Design in the
Pinakothek der
Moderne, Munich

CLIENT
Die Neue Sammlung,
Staatliches Museum für
angewandte Kunst –
Design in der
Pinakothek der
Moderne, Munich

APPEARED IN
2003

DESIGN
bangertprojects
Albrecht Bangert
Munich/Schopfheim
Realisation and
engineering:
durlum Decke Licht
Raum, Schopfheim

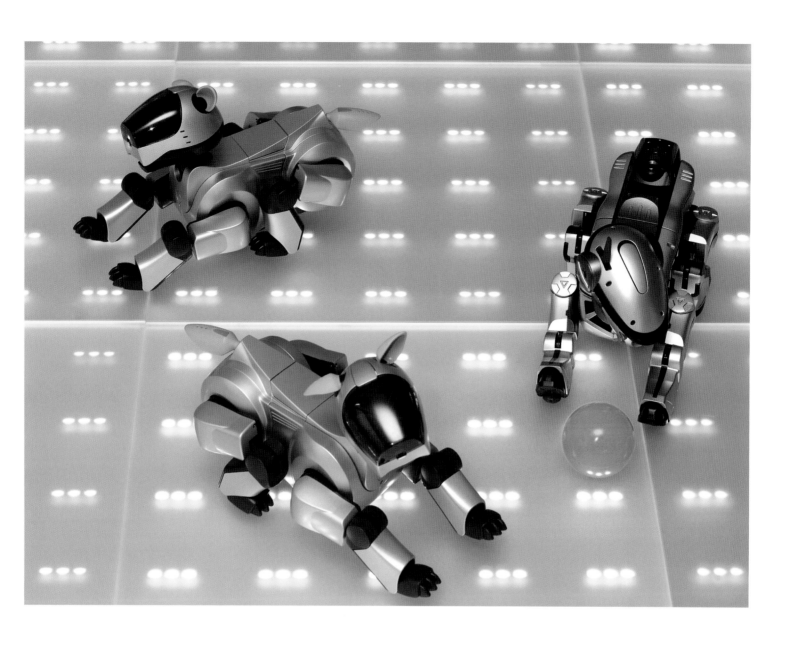

TITLE
Aquademie
Hansgrohe AG

TYPE OF WORK
Showroom

CLIENT
Hansgrohe AG,
Schiltach

DESIGN
fön,design_
arkas förstner,
Schramberg

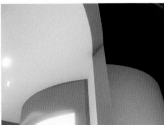

TITLE
iTUBE

TYPE OF WORK
Mobile interactive
architecture,
interface design

APPEARED IN
07|2003

DESIGN
Peyote cross
design concepts,
Vienna, Kufstein
Oliver Irschitz

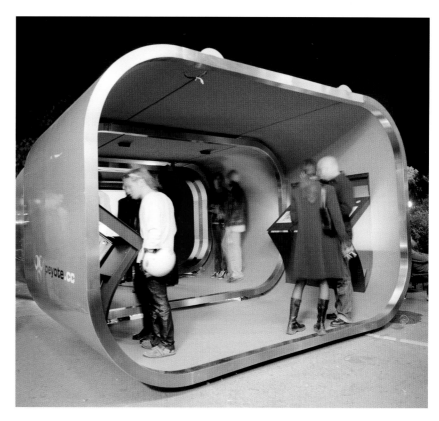

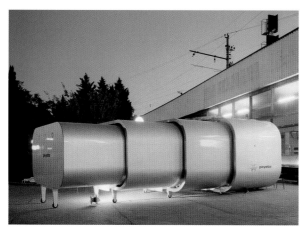

TITLE
Illumination:
Evolution,
Luminale 2004

TYPE OF WORK
Media installation +
exhibition

APPEARED IN
04|2004

DESIGN
Atelier Markgraph,
Frankfurt
in cooperation with:
235 Media, Cologne
FOUR TO ONE: scale
design, Hürth
Group.IE, Frankfurt
Schleuse 15, Frankfurt
Senckenberg, Frankfurt
SHOWTEC, Cologne

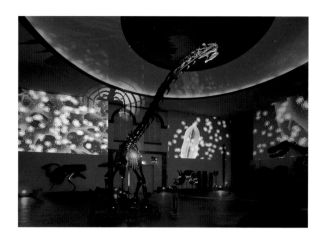

TITLE
Nike Tech Stories:
DriFit

TYPE OF WORK
Retail film

CLIENT
Nike EMEA,
Hilversum

APPEARED IN
10|2003

DESIGN
PostPanic, Amsterdam

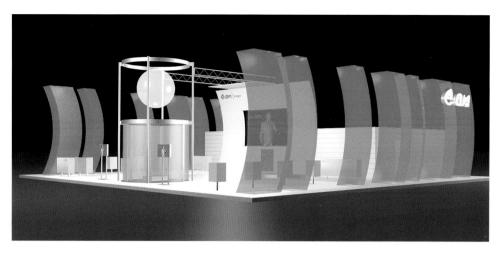

TITLE
E.ON – Bodyscanning

TYPE OF WORK
Trade fair
communication

CLIENT
E.ON Energie, Munich

APPEARED IN
04|2003

DESIGN
Milla und Partner GmbH,
Stuttgart
Schmidhuber + Kaindl,
Munich
Martin Buecker,
Stuttgart

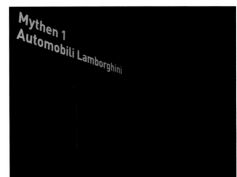

TITLE
Mythen. Automobili
Lamborghini

TYPE OF WORK
Exhibition design

CLIENT
Die Neue Sammlung,
Design in der Pinako-
thek der Moderne,
Munich

APPEARED IN
06|2004 – 07|2004

DESIGN
KMS Team GmbH,
Munich
Creative direction/
curator:
Michael Keller
Art direction:
Birgit Vogel
Text: Axel Sanjosé
Technical direction:
Wahan Mechitarian
Film: Dirk Koy
Poster design:
Birgit Vogel,
Marion Fink
Lighting concept:
Klaus Dilger
Project management:
Armin Schlamp,
Eva Rohrer,
Andreas Koch
Production:
Christina Baur,
Melanie Sauer

TITLE
XBox-Lounge

TYPE OF WORK
Corporate interior
design

CLIENT
Microsoft
Deutschland GmbH,
Unterschleißheim

DESIGN
feldmann+schultchen
design, Hamburg

TYPE OF WORK

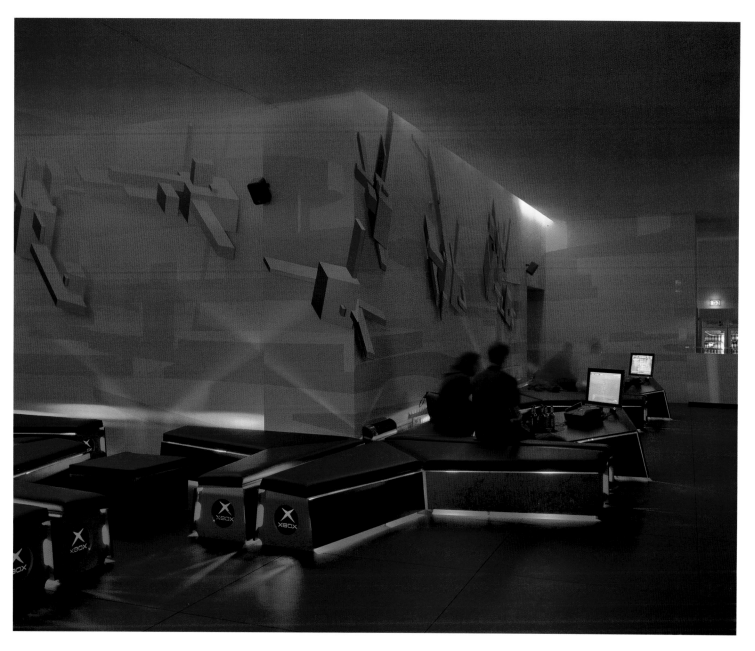

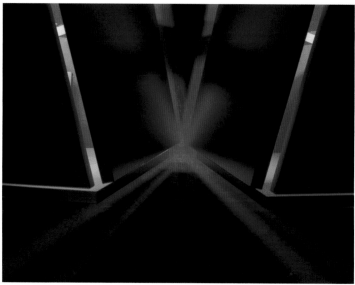

RED DOT WERTDRUCKSACHEN
Scheckkarten | Telefonkarten | Briefmarken | Urkunden | Wertpapiere
Banknoten | Sonstiges

RED DOT PRINTED VALUABLES

Cheque Cards | Telephone Cards | Postage Stamps | Certificates | Securities
Banknotes | Others

Jury:
Jean Jacques Schaffner
Frido Steinen-Broo
Stefan Ytterborn

TITLE
Poster-Art

TYPE OF WORK
Commemorative
stamp

CLIENT
Bundesministerium
der Finanzen, Berlin

APPEARED IN
05|2003

DESIGN
Christof Gassner,
Darmstadt

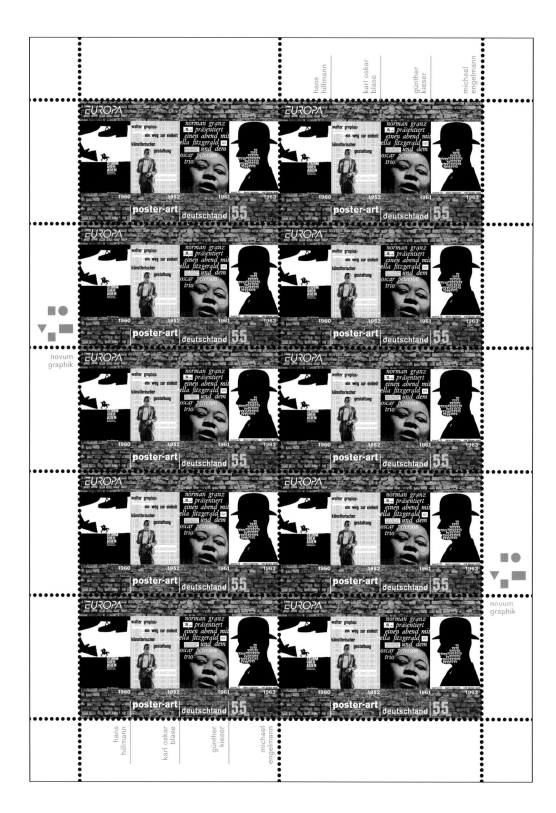

Handle so, daß die Wirkungen deiner
Handlungen verträglich sind mit
der Permanenz echten menschlichen
Lebens auf Erden.

Deutschland   Hans Jonas 1903 - 1993

220

100 Jahre   Katholischer Deutscher Frauenbund

Deutschland **55**

Deutschland

55   Heiliger Bonifatius
       † 754

TITLE
100. Geburtstag
Hans Jonas,
Heiliger Bonifatius,
100 Jahre Katho-
lischer Deutscher
Frauenbund

TYPE OF WORK
Postage stamps

CLIENT
Bundesministerium
der Finanzen, Berlin

APPEARED IN
05|2003–05|2004

DESIGN
Lutz Menze Design,
Wuppertal
Lutz Menze

RED DOT SPORT UND VERANSTALTUNGEN, KUNST UND KULTUR
Plakate | Einladungen | Ankündigungen | Kataloge | Erscheinungsbilder | Signets | Sonstiges

RED DOT SPORTS AND EVENTS, ART AND CULTURE
Posters | Invitations | Announcements | Catalogues | Public Image | Signets | Others

Jury:
Mervyn Kurlansky
Guy Schockaert
Kurt Weidemann

RUHRtriennale 02 03 04
Künstlerischer Leiter Gerard Mortier

Saison 2004

TIERNO BOKAR

NACH DEM WERK VON AMADOU HAMPÂTÉ BÂ (1901–1999)
BEARBEITET VON MARIE-HÉLÈNE ESTIENNE UND PETER BROOK
URAUFFÜHRUNG

REGIE Peter Brook
TEXTBEARBEITUNG
Marie-Hélène Estienne
Peter Brook

TIERNO BOKAR BEGAB SICH stets in schwierige Situationen, um zu prüfen, ob er selbst die Ausdauer besäße, die er andere lehrte. Eines Tages sprach er: ,Ich bitte Gott darum, dass ich im Moment meines Todes mehr Feinde habe, denen ich niemals etwas zuleide tat, als Freunde. Ich interessiere mich nur für jenen Kampf, der auf unsere inneren Schwächen abzielt. Dieser Kampf hat nichts zu tun mit dem Krieg, den die Söhne Adams im Namen eines Gottes führen, von dem sie behaupten, ihn sehr zu lieben, ihn aber wenig lieben, da sie einen Teil seines Werkes zerstören.'
Wer war Tierno Bokar? Der afrikanische Schriftsteller Amadou Hampâté Bâ erzählt uns in seinem Werk *Der Weise von Bandiagara* vom Leben und der Lehre seines

Meisters, eines bescheidenen und außergewöhnlichen Mannes. Die Erzählung führt uns in ein traditionelles und animistisches Afrika, das vom Islam geprägt und von den Kämpfen des Kolonialismus erschüttert ist. Das von Marie-Hélène Estienne und mir nach Amadou Hampâté Bâs Erzählung geschriebene Theaterstück spricht mehr denn je ein Thema an, das unsere gesamte heutige Welt betrifft: Gewalt und Intoleranz. Theater muss sehr nahe an uns sein, um uns anzusprechen – und sehr unerwartet, um unsere Phantasie zu wecken. *Tierno Bokar* vereinigt diese zwei Bedingungen in sich. Peter Brook

GEBLÄSEHALLE
LANDSCHAFTSPARK DUISBURG-NORD
PREMIERE 6. JULI
VORSTELLUNGEN
7., 8., 9., 13., 11., 12., 14., 15., 17. JULI
BEGINN 20 UHR
(16., 17. JULI 16 UHR)
DAUER DER VORSTELLUNG
2 STUNDEN 30 MIN., KEINE PAUSE

In französischer Sprache
mit deutschen Übertiteln.

Dieses Projekt wird gefördert von der
Kunststiftung NRW

Koproduktion mit dem C.I.C.T / Théâtre des Bouffes du Nord, Paris; dem Forum Universal de las Culturas – Barcelona 04; dem Théâtre du Nord – Théâtre National Lille Tourcoing Région Nord Pas-de-Calais avec Lille 2004 – Capitale Européenne de la Culture und der Associazione Teatro Stabile di Napoli.

RAUM.PFAD

MAN MÖCHTE SICH MANCHMAL FRAGEN, OB MAN AUF DEM
RICHTIGEN PLANETEN IST. SAMUEL BECKETT

MARSFIEBER UND MONDSÜCHTIG: Menschen berauschen sich an der Unendlichkeit des Universums und träumen von neuen Welten, vielleicht auf der anderen Seite des Mondes, vielleicht auf dem Mars. Neue Hoffnungen, neues Glück. Glück auf. Das 20. Jahrhundert hat Utopien gründlich diskreditiert. Die letzte ist die vom Mann im Mond, die uns genommen wird, als die ersten Menschen auf dem Mond einen großen Schritt für die Menschheit tun. Sie blicken von fern auf die Erde – und wir wissen nicht mehr, wohin die Reise uns noch führen soll. Auf den Mars? Und weiter? Von nun an wissen wir nicht mehr, was wir glauben sollen. Und schon gar nicht mehr, wo wir sind. Wir rauschen durch Ströme von Sounds und Symbolen, von Bildern und Informationen, taumeln durch Räume

und versinken in Kapitalströmen. Kein Ort, nirgends. Aber wenn die Utopien im Fernsehen sind und die Oberfläche des Mars' jetzt auch im Netz, dann müssen wir die ganz anderen Orte woanders suchen, Utopien sind Räume ohne Ort. Sie sind im Kopf und nicht im Fernsehen. Am Ende kosmologischer Abenteuer und intellektueller Expeditionen ins Nichts führt *Raum.Pfad* zurück auf den Boden und schlägt sich durchs Dickicht der Städte. *Raum.Pfad* führt zu vier Orten mitten im Ruhrgebiet, die ganz anders sind, als das, was sie sein sollen. Vier Projekte erkunden den Raum zwischen Himmel und Erde, Wildnis und Stadt, Stillstand und Bewegung, zwischen Schein und Realität.
KÜNSTLERISCHE LEITUNG Holger Bergmann
PROJEKTDRAMATURGIE Sabine Resch

RAUM.PFAD – 1 OEDIPUS RELOADED
Medienperformance von Klaus Obermaier
In der interaktiven Rauminstallation befragt Ödipus die fließenden Grenzen zwischen Schein und Realität, Wissen, Glauben und Erinnerung. Verloren irrt er im Netz der High-Tech-Daten, geblendet von Bildern und Informationen. Ödipus, der erste Forschungsreisende, der nicht wusste, wo er ist.
RINGLOKSCHUPPEN MÜLHEIM
VORSTELLUNGEN 2., 3., 4., 5., 6., 8., 9. JUNI
BEGINN 20 UHR

RAUM.PFAD – 2 BEING JEKYLL & HYDE
Theaternacht mit Musik von *hören und der club of gore*. Regie: Michael Witte
Das Parkhaus ist kein Ort, sondern ein Zustand. Ein Zustand zwischen zwei Orten, in dem man stehen bleibt, obwohl man eigentlich unterwegs ist. Niemand will in ein Parkhaus. Ein Parkhaus ist ein Zustand, in dem jede Selbsterkenntnis zur Horror-Story wird: Dein Auto ist der einzige Ort, der dir bleibt.
BERMUDA3ECK, PARKHAUS EBENE 3,
BOCHUM
VORSTELLUNGEN 18., 19., 20., 22., 23., 24., 25., 26. JUNI, BEGINN 21 UHR

RAUM.PFAD – 3 SPARTACUS III
Tanztheater-Choreographie: Mark Sieczkarek
Im Niemandsland des gescheiterten Bauprojekts am Rande der Stadt führt der Weg des Spartacus. Ode: schlammig, matschig, zwischen Unkraut und Subkultur endet der Rebellion im verzweifelten Überlebenskampf des Einzelnen. Befreiung oder Selbstverwirklichung? Sehnsucht oder Sucht?

BERLINER PLATZ, ESSEN
VORSTELLUNGEN 7., 8., 9., 10., 11. JULI
BEGINN 21 UHR

RAUM.PFAD – 4 DER MANN VON OBEN
Ein dramatischer Aufbruch zum Mond
Regie: Albrecht Hirche
Auf dem Dach eines Hochhauses richtet sich der Blick in den Himmel. Was erwarten wir, wenn wir nach oben schauen? Eine Antwort? Eine Frage? Außerirdische, die uns abholen? Den Mann im Mond? Wie hoch oben können wir uns einrichten, ohne zu fallen?
SWB-HOCHHAUS, HANS-BÖCKLER-PLATZ,
MÜLHEIM
VORSTELLUNGEN 14., 15., 16., 17., 18., 20., 21., 22., 23. JULI, BEGINN 21 UHR

WEITERE VERANSTALTUNGEN:
FÜR EINE PHILOSOPHIE DER RAUMSTATION
Die Absolute Insel, Vortrag von Peter Sloterdijk & *Out of the Präsent*, ein Film von Andrei Ujica
JAHRHUNDERTHALLE BOCHUM
VERANSTALTUNG 20. MAI, BEGINN 20 UHR

„BACK TO EARTH"-PARTY
Bodenstation
RINGLOKSCHUPPEN MÜLHEIM
VERANSTALTUNG 23. JULI
BEGINN 21 UHR

Koproduktion der RuhrTriennale mit dem Ringlokschuppen Mülheim

Weitere Informationen unter www.ringlokschuppen.de oder T: 0208.99160

Die Wiedererrichtung des Himmels

TITLE
RuhrTriennale
Jahresprogramm 2004

TYPE OF WORK
Book

CLIENT
Klartext Verlagsgesellschaft mbH, Essen

APPEARED IN
06 | 2004

DESIGN
Oktober Kommunikationsdesign GmbH,
Bochum
Katharina Mechow,
Silke Löhmann,
René Wynands
Photography:
Gerhard Richter

TITLE
rausgegenzt.

TYPE OF WORK
Polit-Design

CLIENT
serres, design.
Hattingen

APPEARED IN
04|2004

DESIGN
serres, design.
Hattingen
Thomas Serres

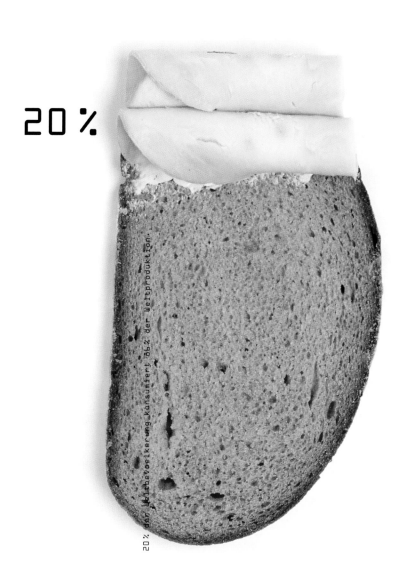

20 % der Weltbevoelkerung konsumiert 86 % der Weltproduktion.

20 %

-> gegen globale Armut : www.aktionsprogramm2015.de

TITLE
"20%" – Plakat-
wettbewerb "Farbe
bekennen. Gegen
globale Armut."
Aktionsprogramm
2015
(junior award)

TYPE OF WORK
Poster

CLIENT
Bundesministerium
für wirtschaftliche
Zusammenarbeit und
Entwicklung, Bonn

APPEARED IN
03|2004

DESIGN
Andreas Stiller,
Wuppertal

TITLE
im Schtei – Plakatserie
(with distinction)
(junior award)

TYPE OF WORK
50 event posters

CLIENT
Kulturkeller im Schtei,
Sempach

DESIGN
Erich Brechbühl
[Mixer], Luzern

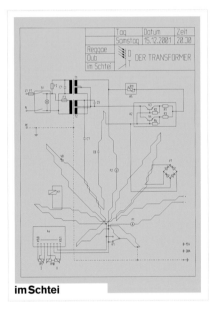

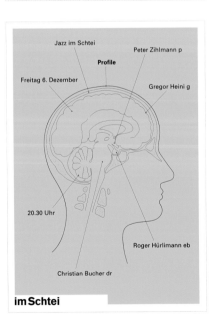

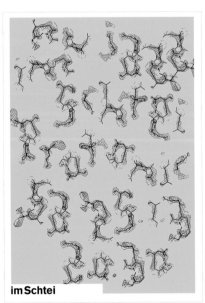

im Schtei

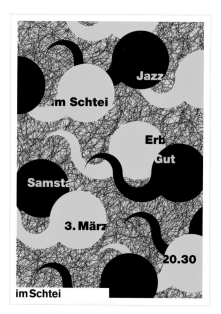

im Schtei

im Schtei

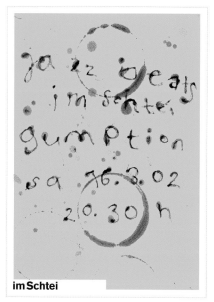

im Schtei

im Schtei

im Schtei

im Schtei

im Schtei

im Schtei

TITLE
Metamorphose

TYPE OF WORK
Poster

CLIENT
Studio für Fotografie
Markus Steur,
Dortmund

APPEARED IN
2003

DESIGN
Fons Hickmann m23
GmbH, Berlin
Simon Gallus,
Fons Hickmann
Photography:
Studio für Fotografie
Markus Steur,
Dortmund

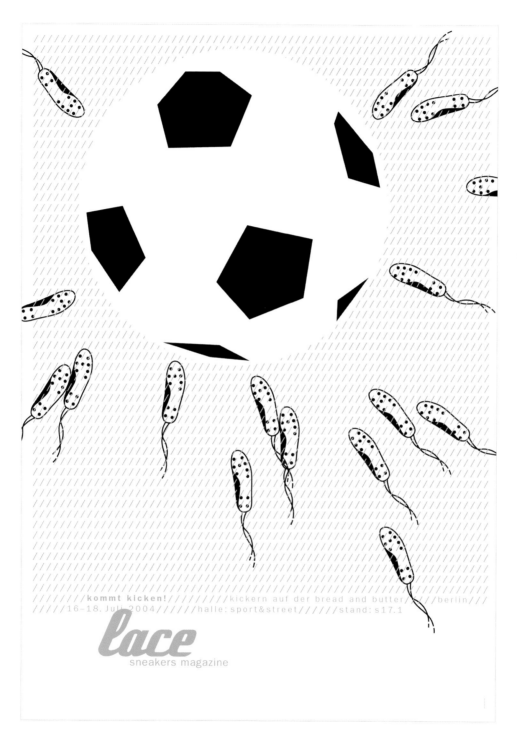

TITLE
Kommt Kicken!
(junior award)

TYPE OF WORK
Poster

CLIENT
Lace
Sneakers Magazine,
Mülheim a. d. Ruhr

APPEARED IN
06|2004

DESIGN
smakdesign,
Duisburg
Marcus Chwalczyk

TITLE
Add. 17469.
A Little Dust
Whispered

TYPE OF WORK
Book

CLIENT
British Library,
London

APPEARED IN
05|2004

DESIGN
Eggers + Diaper,
Berlin
Mark Diaper

Add. 17469
A Little Dust Whispered
Rachel Lichtenstein

Add. 70931

This is a select manuscript that arrived on my desk boxed in green leather with a gold trim. I carefully opened it up and extracted the travelogue. A librarian wandered past at regular intervals, throwing me a backward glance every now and then. Inside the front cover '£7500' is written in pencil and I wondered if the diary has been bought by the Library in an auction or donated. Every page of the book is covered in shaky handwriting from a thick-nibbed blue ink pen. The writing is orderly but almost impossible to decipher as if it has been deliberately written in code like Leonardo da Vinci's notebooks. I struggled to read it for over an hour, managing only to pick out single words like 'heat', 'drinking', 'Havana', 'prostitutes' and 'bed', the words creating an aura of violence and danger in a distant, exotic location. I wondered if his writing is a reflection of inner turmoil or whether he learnt how to write like this during his time as an MI6 spy. Maybe it's a coded form of personal shorthand to protect his writing from someone like me, trying to read his private, unpublished thoughts. It's something I often think about whilst researching in the manuscripts room. Is it morally right for any reader to be able to leaf through the private journals and diaries of those long dead, who almost certainly never intended for these documents to be made public property? Out of a desire to protect his privacy I have decided to photograph a tiny section of his nearly illegible handwriting which transforms into a series of painterly marks. R.L.

Detail from Graham Greene's diary entitled *A Few Final Journeys*, recording travels to Panama, Nicaragua, Russia and Spain, and including notes relating to his novel *The Captain and the Enemy*, 1986–1987. [VOL. II, F. 21, p. 17]

[illus. opposite]

Add. 70931

Through the magnifying glass, the marks on the paper take on their own landscape.

Add. 48210

Add. 37448

I spent a considerable amount of time looking through a number of Hekekyan's journals. They are just such beautiful objects. The style and quality of the author's handiwork is exquisite, particularly, in my opinion, his Arabic script. Sadly, recent world news events have changed the potential meaning of a page of unknown Arabic writing.

I tried to get this particular page translated but the task proved nearly impossible as bookworms have literally eaten away so much of the text that its meaning can no longer be recovered. The intervention of paper conservators to stop the process of time and decay destroying this page completely can be felt more than visibly seen. Covering the surface of the page is a film of mesh-like fabric finer than a butterfly's wing that is literally holding the fragments of the page together. Seeing the skill involved in the repair of this book inspired me to visit the Conservation Department of the British Library where I spent an incredible day taking photographs of and talking to conservators at work. They showed me frail leaves of manuscripts that had been carefully washed and were drying on beds of hand-made papers. I saw a broken wooden binding painstakingly repaired with brass pins, and a tiny, ancient Somalian prayer book worn by monks in a minute, heavily stitched leather satchel. The satchel proved too fragile to be repaired and the conservator who showed it to me had spent weeks constructing a handmade box for it to rest in, filled with soft padded cushions. R.L.

Autobiography written on a voyage to Egypt by Joseph Hekekyan Bey, an Egyptian in the Armenian service, 1830. [VOL. I, p. 456]

[illus. opposite]

Add. 37448

258

svjetlo

Dom likovnih umjetnika Ivan Meštrović
Galerija Prsten i Galerija PM
26.03. - 10.05.2003.

hdlu

DAVOR ANTOLIĆ ANTAS   IVAN FAKTOR   IVANA FRANKE   ANTO JERKOVIĆ   MLADEN GALIĆ

JULIJE KNIFER   IVAN MARUŠIĆ KLIF   ANTUN MOTIKA   MAGDALENA PEDERIN   GORAN PETERCOL

VESNA POKAS   DUBRAVKA RAKOCI   DAMIR SOKIĆ   ALEKSANDAR SRNEC   LJERKA ŠIBENIK

SLAVEN TOLJ   KSENIJA TURČIĆ   MIRJANA VODOPIJA   VLADO ZRNIĆ   SISLEJ XHAFA

Pod pokroviteljstvom Ministarstva kulture RH i Gradskog ureda za kulturu Grada Zagreba.   Sponzori: UNIQA / IGEPA - Plana papiri / OSRAM / UNIJA Zajednica Albanaca Hrvatske / TEP / HSM

TITLE
Light

TYPE OF WORK
Exhibition poster

CLIENT
HDLU, Zagreb

APPEARED IN
03|2003

DESIGN
Laboratorium,
Zagreb
Orsat Franković,
Ivana Vučić

TITLE
BB3

TYPE OF WORK
Event design

CLIENT
3. Berlin Biennale

APPEARED IN
02|2004 – 04|2004

DESIGN
Novamondo Design,
Berlin
Matthias Gau,
Bastian Köhler,
Christian Schlimok,
Anna Löwen,
Chris Steurer

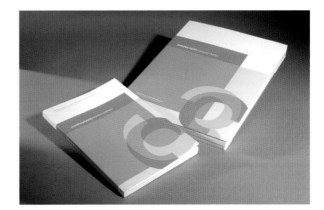

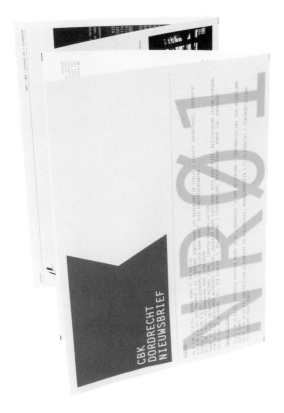

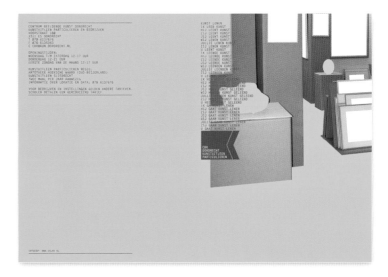

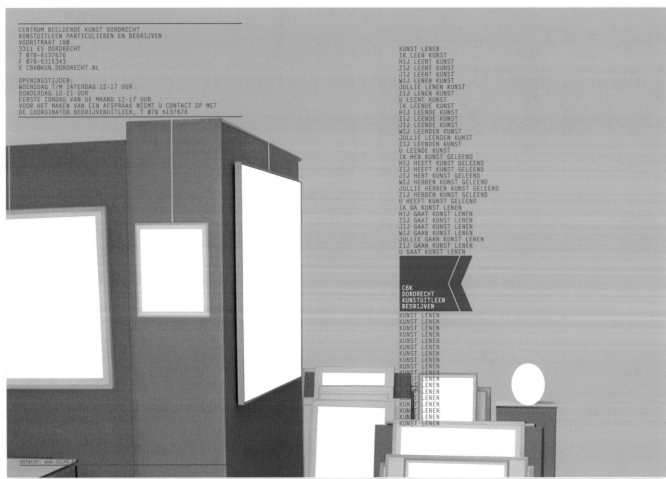

CENTRUM BEELDENDE KUNST DORDRECHT
KUNSTUITLEEN PARTICULIEREN EN BEDRIJVEN
VOORSTRAAT 180
3311 ES DORDRECHT
T 078-6137676
F 078-6315343
E CBK@KUN.DORDRECHT.NL

OPENINGSTIJDEN:
WOENSDAG T/M ZATERDAG 12-17 UUR
DONDERDAG 12-21 UUR
EERSTE ZONDAG VAN DE MAAND 12-17 UUR
VOOR HET MAKEN VAN DE EEN AFSPRAAK NEEMT U CONTACT OP MET
DE COORDINATOR BEDRIJVENUITLEEN, T 078 6137676

KUNST LENEN
IK LEEN KUNST
HIJ LEENT KUNST
ZIJ LEENT KUNST
JIJ LEENT KUNST
WIJ LENEN KUNST
JULLIE LENEN KUNST
ZIJ LENEN KUNST
U LEENT KUNST
IK LEENDE KUNST
HIJ LEENDE KUNST
ZIJ LEENDE KUNST
JIJ LEENDE KUNST
WIJ LEENDEN KUNST
JULLIE LEENDEN KUNST
ZIJ LEENDEN KUNST
U LEENDE KUNST
IK HEB KUNST GELEEND
HIJ HEEFT KUNST GELEEND
ZIJ HEEFT KUNST GELEEND
JIJ HEBT KUNST GELEEND
WIJ HEBBEN KUNST GELEEND
JULLIE HEBBEN KUNST GELEEND
ZIJ HEBBEN KUNST GELEEND
U HEEFT KUNST GELEEND
IK GA KUNST LENEN
HIJ GAAT KUNST LENEN
ZIJ GAAT KUNST LENEN
JIJ GAAT KUNST LENEN
WIJ GAAN KUNST LENEN
JULLIE GAAN KUNST LENEN
ZIJ GAAN KUNST LENEN
U GAAT KUNST LENEN

CBK
DORDRECHT
KUNSTUITLEEN
BEDRIJVEN

KUNST LENEN
KUNST LENEN
KUNST LENEN
KUNST LENEN
KUNST LENEN
KUNST LENEN
KUNST LENEN
KUNST LENEN
KUNST LENEN
KUNST LENEN
KUNST LENEN
KUNST LENEN
KUNST LENEN

ONTWERP: WWW.SOLAR.NL

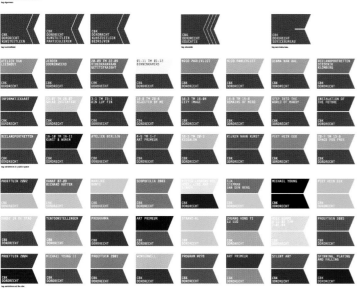

TITLE
Communication
project for Art Centre
CBK Dordrecht

TYPE OF WORK
Communication
project

CLIENT
Centrum Beeldende
Kunst (CBK) Dordrecht

DESIGN
Solar Initiative,
Amsterdam
Miguel Gori, Marieke
Müskens van Bemmel,
Ivo Schmetz, Nelleke
Wegdam, Remco van
Bladel, Stephan
Achterberg

TITLE
Croatia – A world of
difference
The Mediterranean
as it once was

TYPE OF WORK
Posters

CLIENT
Croatian National
Tourist Board, Zagreb

APPEARED IN
05|2004

DESIGN
Studio International
Boris Ljubičić, Zagreb
Photography:
Ivo Pervan

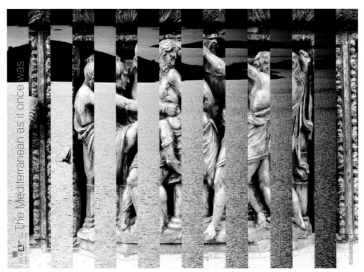

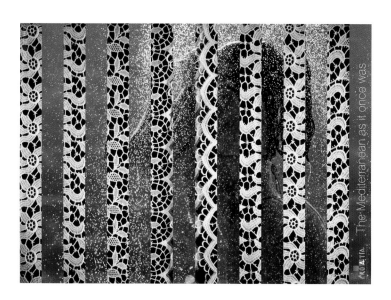

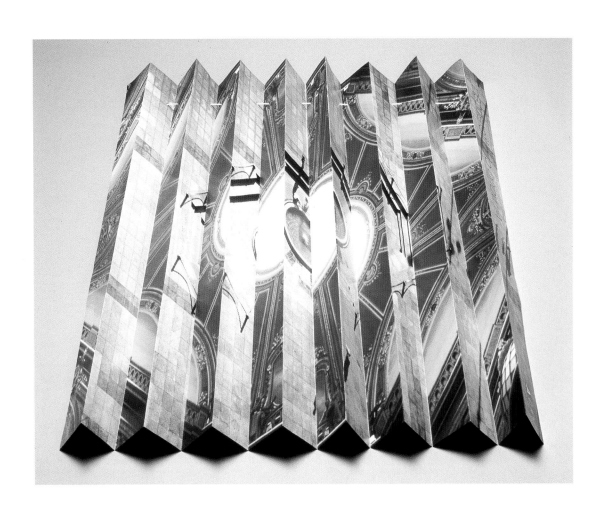

TITLE
Pan & Syrinx.
Eine erotische Jagd

TYPE OF WORK
Catalogue, invitation

CLIENT
Staatliche Museen
Kassel

APPEARED IN
03|2004

DESIGN
Stephanie + Ralf
de Jong, Kassel

TITLE
Ethnic Heritage
Ensemble

TYPE OF WORK
Poster

CLIENT
Jazz in Willisau

APPEARED IN
10|2003

DESIGN
Niklaus Troxler
Design, Willisau
Prof. Niklaus Troxler

TITLE
Corporal Identity,
Body Language
9th Triennial for
Form and Content
Körpersprache
9. Triennale für Form
und Inhalte

TYPE OF WORK
Poster

CLIENT
Museum
of Arts & Design,
New York
Museum
für Angewandte
Kunst,
Frankfurt/Main
Klingspor Museum,
Offenbach

APPEARED IN
08|2003

DESIGN
Prof. Uwe Loesch,
Düsseldorf-Erkrath

TITLE
Uwe Loesch ... nur
Fliegen ist schöner.
Uwe Loesch ... Fly by.

TYPE OF WORK
Poster

CLIENT
PAN kunstforum
niederrhein, Emmerich

APPEARED IN
10|2003

DESIGN
Prof. Uwe Loesch,
Düsseldorf-Erkrath

TITLE
À bientôt. Affiches
de Uwe Loesch
See you. Posters
by Uwe Loesch
(with distinction)

TYPE OF WORK
Poster

CLIENT
Goethe Institut
Inter Nationes
Rabat/Casablanca,
Rabat

APPEARED IN
10|2003

DESIGN
Prof. Uwe Loesch,
Düsseldorf-Erkrath

TITLE
Weegee – The Famous

TYPE OF WORK
Catalogue

CLIENT
Institut für Kultur-
austausch, Tübingen

APPEARED IN
01|2004

DESIGN
L2M3 Kommunikations
Design, Stuttgart
Sascha Lobe,
Kathrin Löser

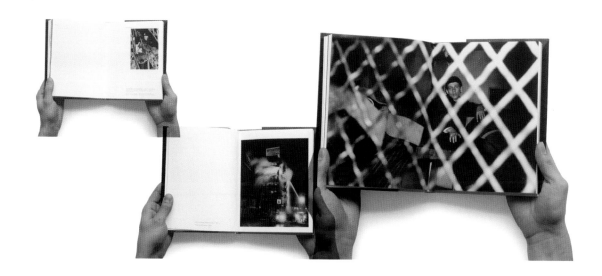

RED DOT PRINTKOMMUNIKATION
Bücher | Kalender | Zeitschriften | Kataloge | Prospekte | Zeitschriftentitel | Zeitschriftenbeiträge
Buchcover | CD-Cover | Fotografie | Typografie (Plakat, Buch etc.) | Illustrationen | Sonstiges

RED DOT **PRINT COMMUNICATION**

Books | Diaries | Magazines | Catalogues | Brochures | Magazine Covers | Magazine Articles | Book Covers
CD Covers | Photography | Typography (Posters, Books etc.) | Illustrations | Others

Jury:
Jean Jacques Schaffner
Frido Steinen-Broo
Stefan Ytterborn

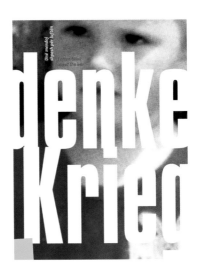

TITLE
Denke Krieg

TYPE OF WORK
Book

CLIENT
MaikäferFlieg e.V.,
Berlin

APPEARED IN
2003

DESIGN
Anna B. Design, Berlin
Anna Berkenbusch,
Tina Wende

Wir haben überlebt, aber wir haben auch erlebt, dass nicht jeder überleben kann.

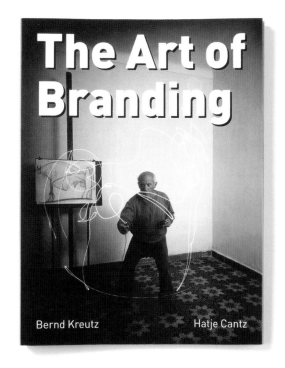

TITLE
Brand Books

TYPE OF WORK
Books

CLIENT
Hatje Cantz Verlag,
Ostfildern

APPEARED IN
10|2003

DESIGN
Kreutz & Partner
Kommunikation,
Düsseldorf
Bernd Kreutz

TITLE
Ruim Baan Voor

TYPE OF WORK
Diaries

CLIENT
Ando bv, The Hague

APPEARED IN
12|2003

DESIGN
Samenwerkende
Ontwerpers bv,
Amsterdam

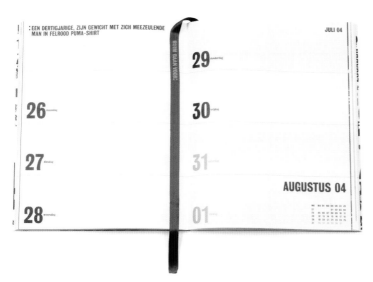

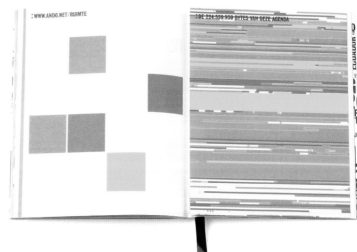

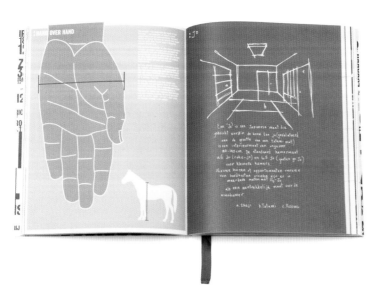

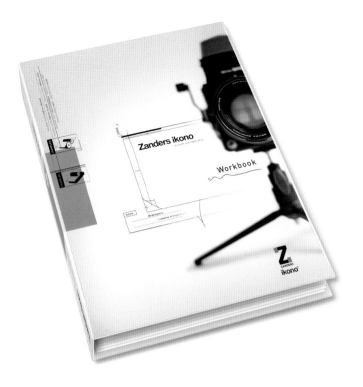

TITLE
Zanders ikono
Workbook

TYPE OF WORK
Book

CLIENT
M-real Zanders GmbH,
Bergisch Gladbach

APPEARED IN
01|2004

DESIGN
BRANDIT
Marketing und
Kommunikation,
Cologne
Peter Specht,
Petra Steuns,
Angela Strecker

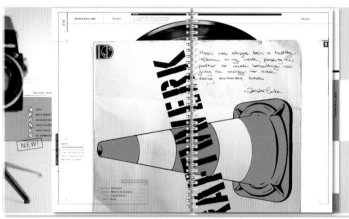

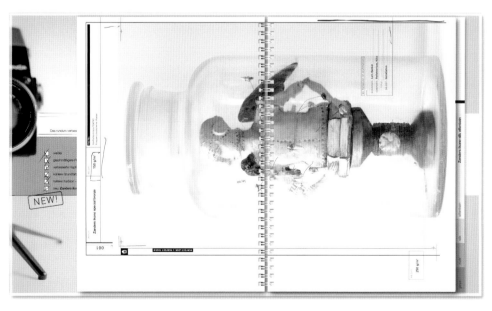

TITLE
Diary 2003

TYPE OF WORK
Diary

CLIENT
Hexspoor, Ferrill,
Grafisch Papier, Quay,
Una, Veenman

APPEARED IN
12/2002

DESIGN
UNA (Amsterdam)
designers, Amsterdam

TITLE
Diary 2004

TYPE OF WORK
Diary

CLIENT
Hexspoor, Ferrill,
Grafisch Papier,
Mart.Spruijt, Una

APPEARED IN
12/2003

DESIGN
UNA (Amsterdam)
designers, Amsterdam

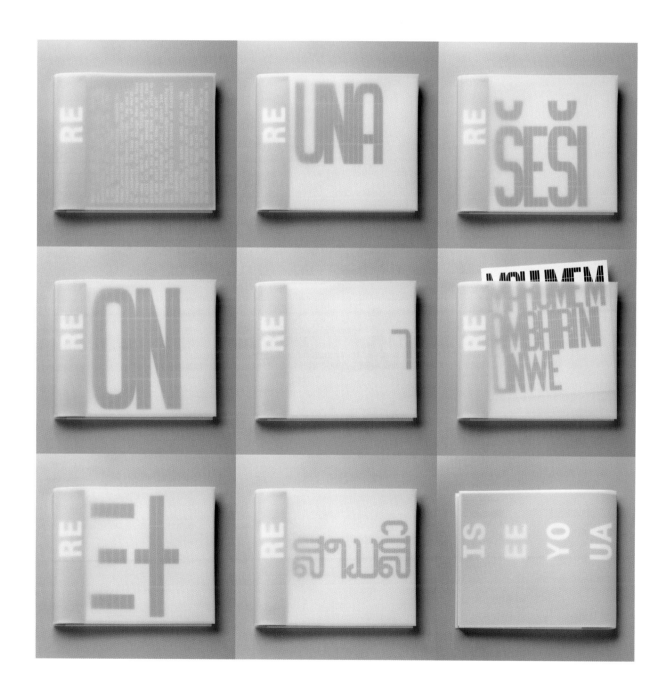

TITLE
Designszene Berlin

TYPE OF WORK
Book

CLIENT
Internationales
Design Zentrum
Berlin (IDZ), Berlin

APPEARED IN
11|2003

DESIGN
kognito gestaltung,
Berlin
David Skopec,
Nanette Amann

TITLE
Landesgeschichten

TYPE OF WORK
Exhibition catalogue

CLIENT
Haus der Geschichte
Baden-Württemberg

APPEARED IN
12|2002

DESIGN
büro diffus GmbH,
Stuttgart

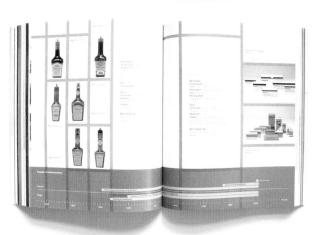

TITLE
Informationen
gestalten

TYPE OF WORK
Book

DESIGN
Prof. Hartmut
Brückner
Büro Brückner +
Partner, Bremen

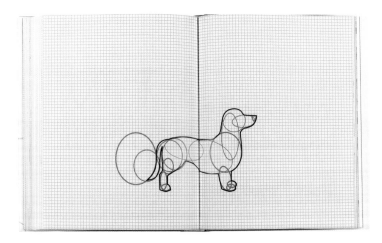

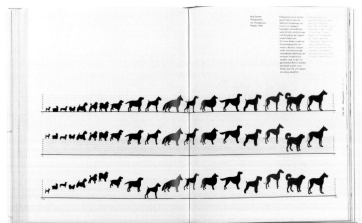

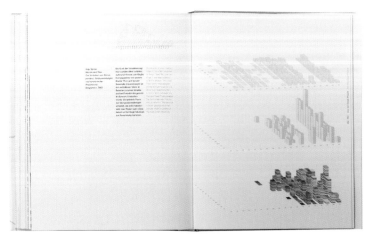

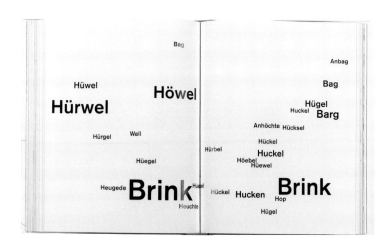

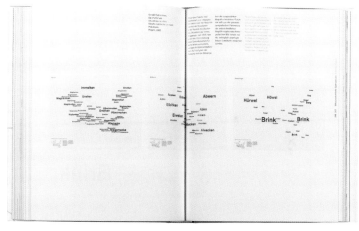

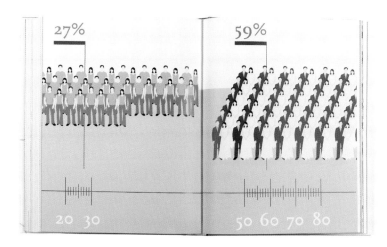

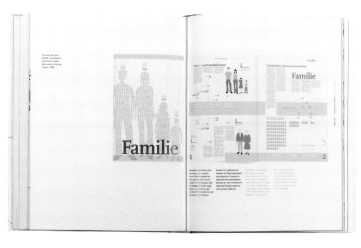

TITLE
Architektur in Baden-
Württemberg 2003

TYPE OF WORK
Book

CLIENT
BDA Bund Deutscher
Architekten, Stuttgart

APPEARED IN
11|2003

DESIGN
büro diffus GmbH,
Stuttgart

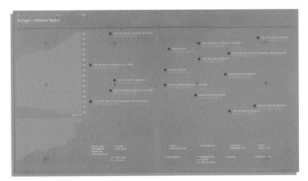

TITLE
Marktplatzbroschüre

TYPE OF WORK
Brochure

CLIENT
Nimbus Design,
Stuttgart

DESIGN
loup.susanne wolf,
Stuttgart
Silke Braun

TITLE
TARA. Armatur und
Archetypus. Eine
Huldigung.

TYPE OF WORK
Book

CLIENT
Aloys F. Dornbracht
GmbH & Co. KG
Armaturenfabrik,
Iserlohn

APPEARED IN
10|2003

DESIGN
Meiré und Meiré AG,
Cologne
Mike Meiré, Katja
Fössel, Kerstin-Anna
Hielscher
Editor in chief:
Thomas Edelmann
Associate editor:
Stephanie Eckerskorn

TITLE
Typografisches
Gedankenspiel

TYPE OF WORK
Playing cards and
packaging for
internal promotion

APPEARED IN
12|2003

DESIGN
Wolfgang Breuninger
Kommunikations-
design, Remseck a. N.

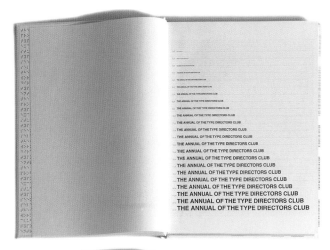

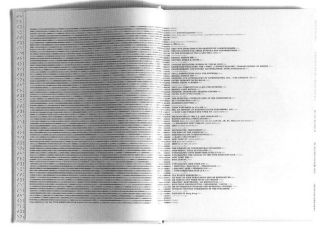

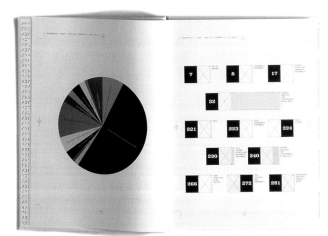

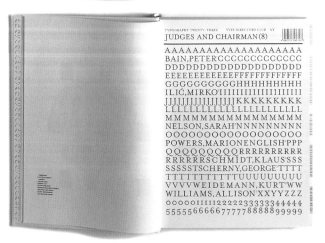

TITLE
Typography 23

TYPE OF WORK
Book

CLIENT
Type Directors Club,
New York

APPEARED IN
01|2003

DESIGN
Design: MW,
New York
Allison Williams,
Anisa Suthalayi

TITLE
Branding Interface
Gespräche über
Markenkommunika-
tion von morgen

TYPE OF WORK
Book

APPEARED IN
03|2004

DESIGN
Martin et Karczinski,
Munich
Peter Martin,
Daniel Karczinski,
Daniela Scharf,
Nicola Sacher,
Andrea Schwabl,
Frank Widemann,
Antje Stumpe,
Beate Mini

TITLE
Plakat zur 50. Type
Directors Show

TYPE OF WORK
Poster

CLIENT
Type Directors Club
of New York, german
liaison committee

APPEARED IN
05|2004

DESIGN
Michaela Burger,
Andreas Uebele,
Sandra Zellmer

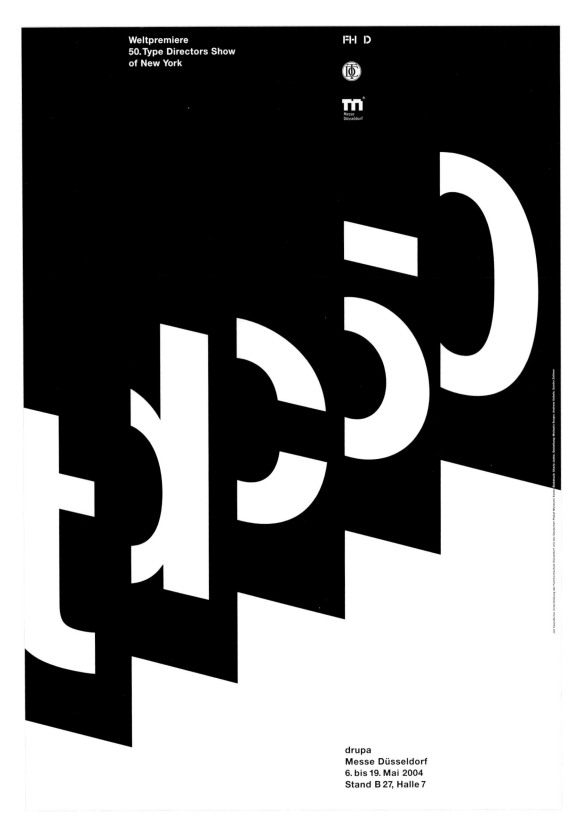

TITLE
"perspectives"

PUBLISHER
Gerd Bulthaup

TYPE OF WORK
Book

CLIENT
Hoffmann und
Campe Verlag GmbH,
Hamburg

APPEARED IN
04 | 2004

DESIGN
Mutabor Design
GmbH, Hamburg
Johannes Plass,
Sven Ritterhoff

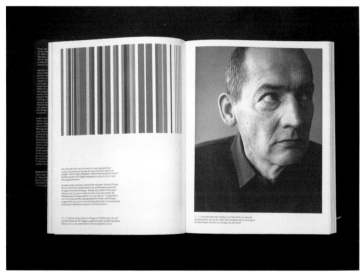

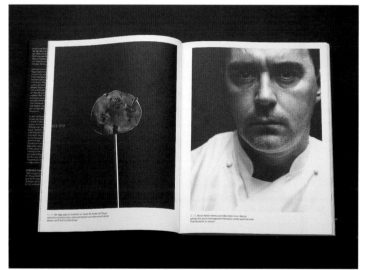

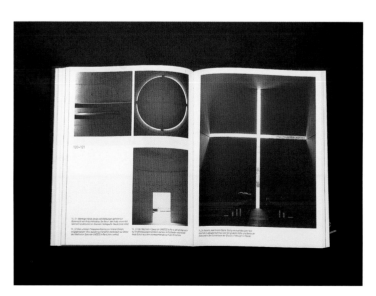

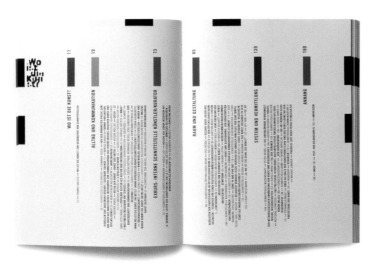

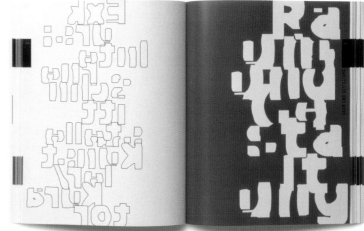

TITLE
Wo ist die Kunst –
Zur Geografie von
Schnittstellen
(junior award)

TYPE OF WORK
Book

CLIENT
Kunstverein
Hildesheim,
Hildesheim

APPEARED IN
03|2004

DESIGN
HAWK Hildesheim
Fachhochschule
Hildesheim/Holzmin-
den/Göttingen
Design faculty,
Hildesheim
Almuth Jung,
Anita Klaiber,
Kerstin Schulz,
Sina Schiewe,
Verena Hirschberger,
Prof. Dominika Hasse

TITLE
"No Money, No Job,
I Drive Taxi."

TYPE OF WORK
Book

CLIENT
Fachhochschule
Düsseldorf
Gerhard Schmal
(supervising professor)

APPEARED IN
02|2004

DESIGN
Judith Wagner,
Düsseldorf

auf der suche nach taxifahrern und ihren träumen fuhr ich 84 tage lang mit dem taxi um die welt. in diesen knapp 3 monaten habe ich 157 taxifahrer kennengelernt, fotografiert und interviewt. auf 8753 meilen taxifahrt habe ich 75 singles, 2 schwule und 23 verheiratete getroffen, 12 christen, 3 moslems, 1 anglikaner, 2 hindus und 1 mohamedaner; in 3 pontiacs, 17 mercedessen, 18 toyotas, 3 nissans, 15 vws, 11 kleinbussen und 1 opel bin ich mitgefaren und in 93 gelben taxis, 28 roten taxis, 9 blauen taxis, 21 schwarzen und 3 orangen taxis habe ich gesessen. davon fuhren mich 5 langhaarige, 79 blonde, 13 mit glaze, 12 schwarze, 57 dunkelhaarige, 3 indios, 35 brillenträger, 15 chinesen, 9 japaner, 1 indianer, 17 linkshänder, 12 mit weissen handschuhen und 41 mit mützen. die fahrer verdienen zwischen 11 pesos, 8 dollar, 3000 riahs, 159 hongkong-dollar, 1099 kronen, 97 us-dollar und 39750 yen am tag.

TITLE
Das Vierte Buch

TYPE OF WORK
Yearbook

CLIENT
Fachhochschule
Wiesbaden
Prof. Gregor Krisztian
(supervising professor)

APPEARED IN
04|2004

DESIGN
Fachhochschule
Wiesbaden
Eugenia Knaub,
Victoria Sarapina,
Sandra Ott,
Nina Hitze,
Georg Dejung

TITLE
Wild West 2004
(junior award)

TYPE OF WORK
Book

CLIENT
Fotostudio Orel,
Stuttgart

APPEARED IN
01|2004

DESIGN
Fotostudio Orel,
Stuttgart
Dennis Orel,
Ingeborg Orel,
Mike Nanz
Volker Hink,
Stuttgart

WINNER

and **Losers**

Teil 1

19 MONTAG

20 DIENSTAG

21 MITTWOCH

22 DONNERSTAG

23 FREITAG

24 SAMSTAG   25 SONNTAG

DIE DALTON-BANDE

Bob, Emmett und Grat Dalton

COW-HORSE-BOOT-LIQUOR

05

THE

LEVI'S

Hosen für den Geldgräber

16 MONTAG

17 DIENSTAG

18 MITTWOCH

19 DONNERSTAG

20 FREITAG

21 SAMSTAG   22 SONNTAG

Plattfüße

DIE RENO-BANDE

15 MONTAG

16 DIENSTAG

17 MITTWOCH

18 DONNERSTAG

19 FREITAG

20 SAMSTAG   21 SONNTAG

SCHIMMELREITER

13 MONTAG

14 DIENSTAG

15 MITTWOCH

16 DONNERSTAG

17 FREITAG

18 SAMSTAG   19 SONNTAG 4. ADVENT

SONNTAGSKIND Auf zum Tanz!

20 MONTAG

21 DIENSTAG

22 MITTWOCH

23 DONNERSTAG

24 FREITAG

25 SAMSTAG 1. WEIHNACHTSTAG   26 SONNTAG 2. WEIHNACHTSTAG

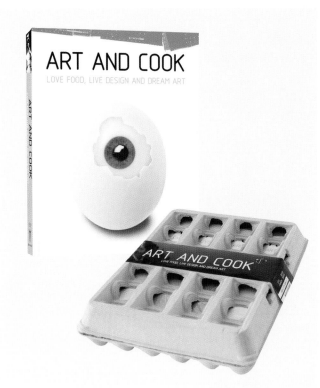

ART AND COOK
LOVE FOOD, LIVE DESIGN AND DREAM ART

**ORANGE AND COGNAC BEEF STEW
OVER EGG NOODLES**
Serves 4

TITLE
Art and Cook

TYPE OF WORK
Cookbook

APPEARED IN
01|2004

DESIGN
Emmanuel Paletz,
New York
Art direction:
Emmanuel Paletz
Design:
Emmanuel Paletz
Photography:
Allan Ben
Recipe developing:
Einav Gefen
Food styling:
Liron Meller,
Melanie R. Underwood

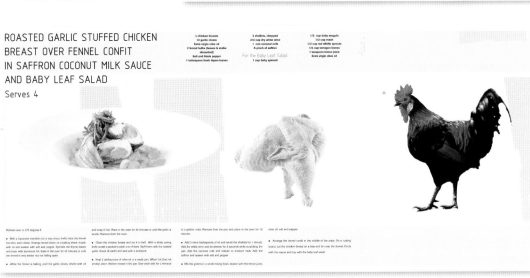

ROASTED GARLIC STUFFED CHICKEN
BREAST OVER FENNEL CONFIT
IN SAFFRON COCONUT MILK SAUCE
AND BABY LEAF SALAD
Serves 4

PAN-SEARED TILAPIA WITH CORNMEAL
CRUST OVER LEEKS, RED PEPPERS
AND POTATO RAGOUT
Serves 4

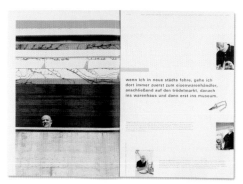

TITLE
so was kommt
von so was
(junior award)

TYPE OF WORK
Magazine,
undergraduate
dissertation

CLIENT
Hochschule für
Künste Bremen

APPEARED IN
07|2003

DESIGN
Siena Jakobi, Bremen
Photography:
Tom Kleiner, Bremen

TITLE
Nachschlag –
430 g Deutschland
(junior award)

TYPE OF WORK
Book, undergraduate
dissertation

CLIENT
Fachhochschule
Düsseldorf
Prof. Victor Malsy,
Prof. Philipp Teufel
(supervising profes-
sors)

APPEARED IN
02|2004

DESIGN
Meike Pöhling,
Düsseldorf

TITLE
VISA oder die Verhin-
derung des Reisens

TYPE OF WORK
Book, poster

CLIENT
IFA Galerie

APPEARED IN
2003

DESIGN
Fons Hickmann m23
GmbH, Berlin
Fons Hickmann,
Barbara Bättig,
Simon Gallus

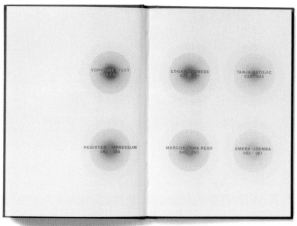

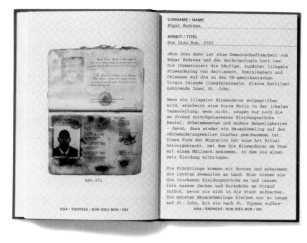

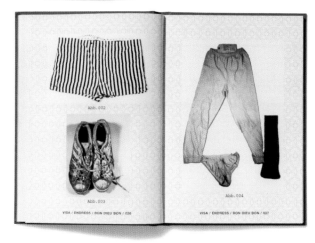

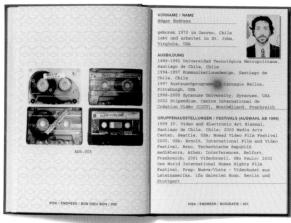

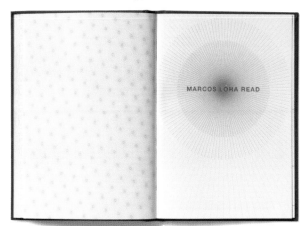

TITLE
open your mind

TYPE OF WORK
Calendar

CLIENT
smart gmbh, Böblingen

APPEARED IN
11|2003

DESIGN
Bruce B. GmbH,
Stuttgart
recom GmbH,
Ostfildern
Creative direction:
Thomas Elser,
Thomas Waschke,
Thorsten Jasper Weese
Photography:
Studio challenge,
smart Archiv

december / dezember / décembre / diciembre / dicembre   1 2 3 4 5 6 7 8 9 10 11 12 13 14 15 16 17 18 19 20 21 22 23 24 25 26 27 28 29 30 31

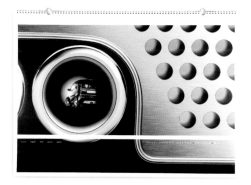

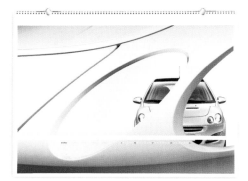

305

TITLE
Am Anfang

TYPE OF WORK
Wissensbuch für
Kinder

CLIENT
Landesmuseum für
Archäologie Sachsen-
Anhalt, Halle/Saale

APPEARED IN
12|2003

DESIGN
burbulla.design,
Berlin
Marion Burbulla

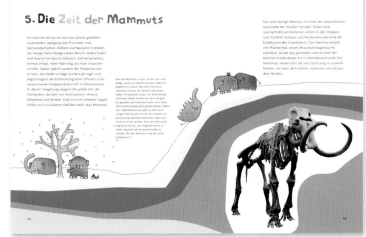

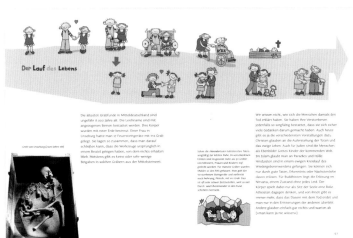

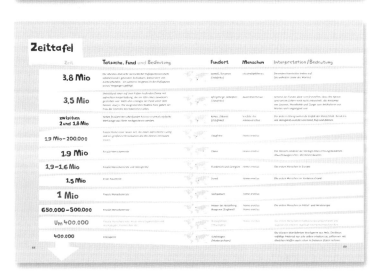

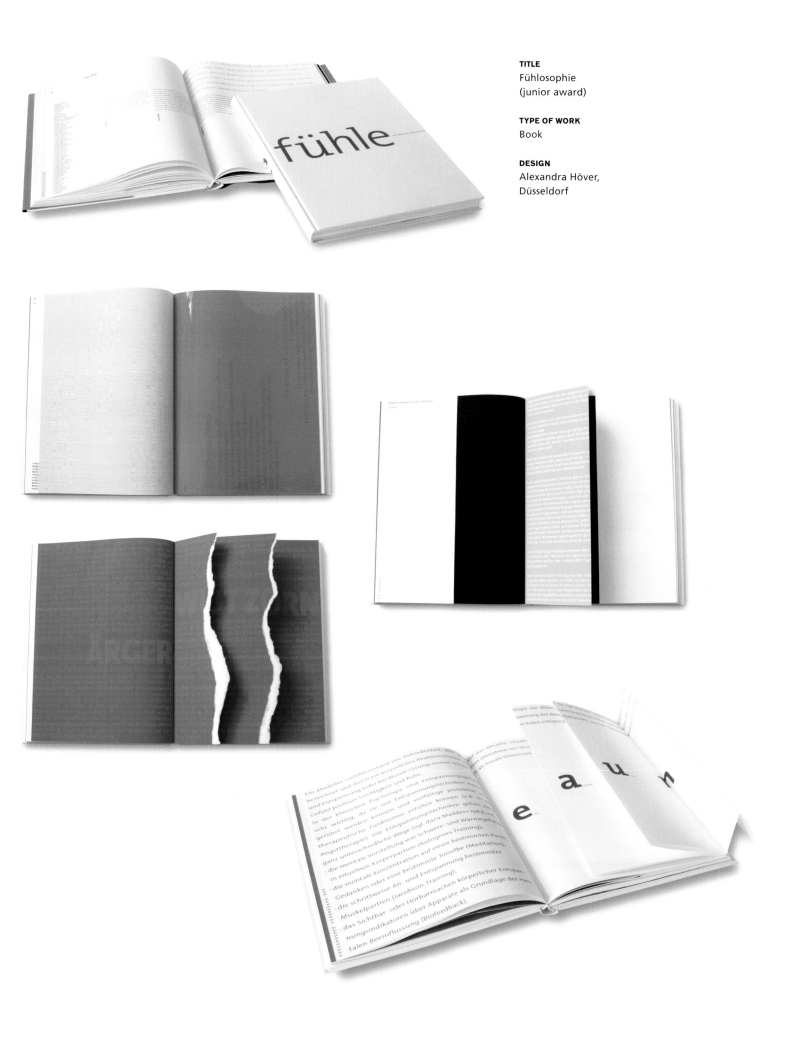

TITLE
Fühlosophie
(junior award)

TYPE OF WORK
Book

DESIGN
Alexandra Höver,
Düsseldorf

TITLE
flush compilation

TYPE OF WORK
CD cover

APPEARED IN
04|2003 – 12|2003

DESIGN
wppt:kommunikation
GmbH, Wuppertal
Rob Fährmann

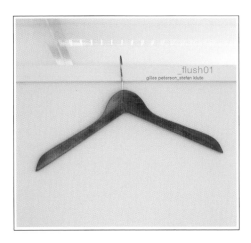

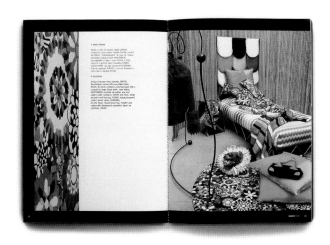

TITLE
Missoni Home

TYPE OF WORK
Brochure

CLIENT
Missoni Spa,
Sumirago
T & J Vestor Spa,
Golasecca
Richard Ginori-
Pagnossin, Treviso

APPEARED IN
01|2004

DESIGN
MMG Srl, Gallarate
Carlo Magnoli

TITLE
In.Kitchen

TYPE OF WORK
Book, CD-ROM,
website

CLIENT
Whirlpool Europe Srl,
Comerio

APPEARED IN
03|2004

DESIGN
MMG Srl, Gallarate
Carlo Magnoli

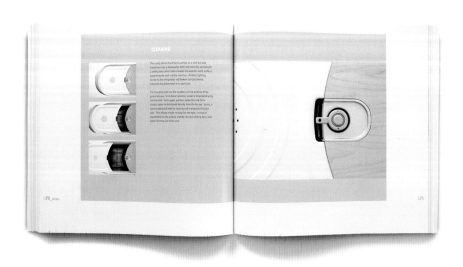

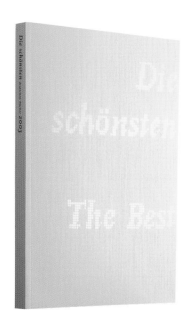

TITLE
Die schönsten
deutschen Bücher 2003
(junior award)

TYPE OF WORK
Book

CLIENT
Stiftung Buchkunst,
Frankfurt am Main
und Leipzig

APPEARED IN
03|2003

DESIGN
Hochschule für Künste
University of the Arts
Bremen
Matthias Wörle,
Emanuela Karantinaki,
Sandra Tebbe,
Jana Frieling
Prof. Eckhard Jung
(supervising professor)

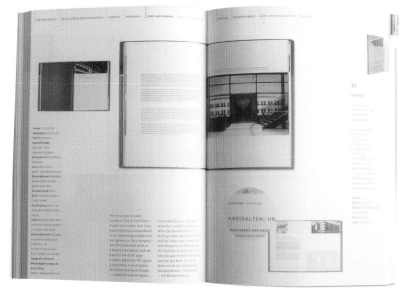

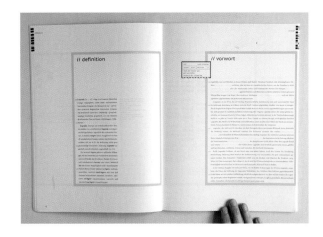

TITLE
"echtzeit 02" Magazin

TYPE OF WORK
Magazine

APPEARED IN
03|2004

DESIGN
Redaktion
"echtzeit 02", Potsdam
Idea and concept:
Svenja von Döhlen,
Steffen Wierer
Published by Fachhoch-
schule Potsdam, design
department

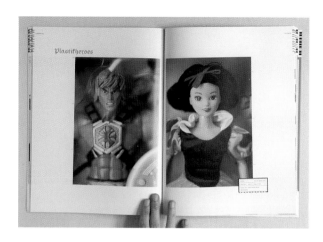

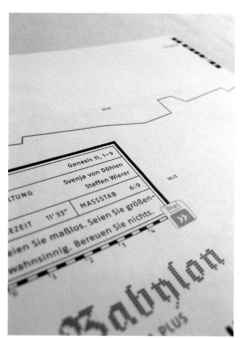

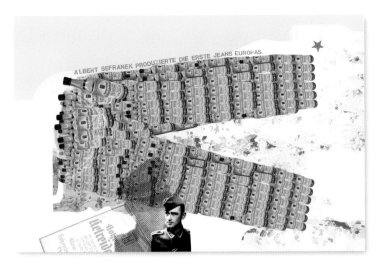

TITLE
Geschichten vom Pferd

TYPE OF WORK
Book

CLIENT
Mustang Jeans GmbH,
Künzelsau

APPEARED IN
07|2003

DESIGN
Springer & Jacoby
Design, Hamburg
Uli Gürtler,
Alexander Rötterink,
Constanze Rusch,
Jens Ringena,
Matthias Storath

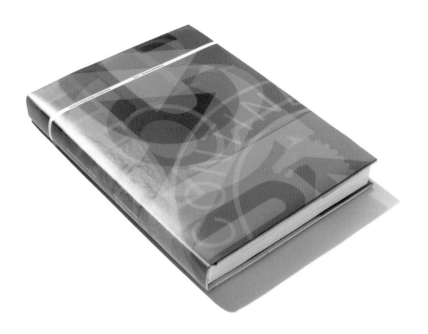

TITLE
Corporate Design-
Kultur in Deutschland
(junior award)

TYPE OF WORK
Book, undergraduate
dissertation

CLIENT
Fachhochschule
Dortmund
Prof. Fons Hickmann,
Barbara Kotte
(supervising profes-
sors)

APPEARED IN
07|2002

DESIGN
Ulf Constantin Stein,
Dortmund

TITLE
Beams T Calendar 2004

TYPE OF WORK
Calendar

CLIENT
Beams Co., Ltd.,
Tokyo

APPEARED IN
2003 – 2004

DESIGN
Hideki Inaba Design,
Tokyo
Hideki Inaba

Sun	Mon	Tue	Wed	Thu	Fri	Sat	Sun	Mon	Tue	Wed	Thu	Fri	Sat
				1	2	3	4	5	6	7	8	9	10
11	12	13	14	15	16	17	18	19	20	21	22	23	24
25	26	27	28	29	30	31	32	33	34	35	36	37	38
39	40	41	42	43	44	45	46	47	48	49	50	51	52
53	54	55	56	57	58	59	60	61	62	63	64	65	66
67	68	69	70	71	72	73	74	75	76	77	78	79	80
81	82	83	84	85	86	87	88	89	90	91	92	93	94
95	96	97	98	99	100	101	102	103	104	105	106	107	108
109	110	111	112	113	114	115	116	117	118	119	120	121	122
123	124	125	126	127	128	129	130	131	132	133	134	135	136
137	138	139	140	141	142	143	144	145	146	147	148	149	150
151	152	153	154	155	156	157	158	159	160	161	162	163	164
165	166	167	168	169	170	171	172	173	174	175	176	177	178
179	180	181	182	183	184	185	186	187	188	189	190	191	192
193	194	195	196	197	198	199	200	201	202	203	204	205	206
207	208	209	210	211	212	213	214	215	216	217	218	219	220
221	222	223	224	225	226	227	228	229	230	231	232	233	234
235	236	237	238	239	240	241	242	243	244	245	246	247	248
249	250	251	252	253	254	255	256	257	258	259	260	261	262
263	264	265	266	267	268	269	270	271	272	273	274	275	276
277	278	279	280	281	282	283	284	285	286	287	288	289	290
291	292	293	294	295	296	297	298	299	300	301	302	303	304
305	306	307	308	309	310	311	312	313	314	315	316	317	318
319	320	321	322	323	324	325	326	327	328	329	330	331	332
333	334	335	336	337	338	339	340	341	342	343	344	345	346
347	348	349	350	351	352	353	354	355	356	357	358	359	360
361	362	363	364	365	366								

2004

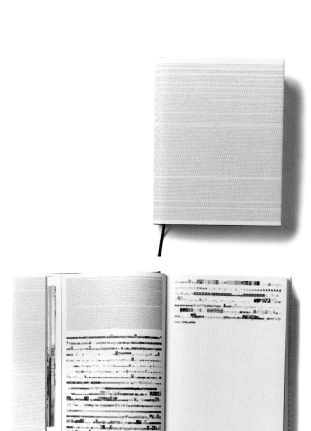

TITLE
D-SIGN
FH Düsseldorf
Infomaterial

TYPE OF WORK
Book, brochure, pamphlet, datasheet

APPEARED IN
02|2004

DESIGN
Fachhochschule
Düsseldorf
Prof. Philipp Teufel,
Prof. Victor Malsy,
Prof. Wilfried
Korfmacher,
Alexander Gialouris,
Thomas Meyer,
Markus Kremer,
Hendrik Bruning,
Nadine Wilms,
Nils Mengedoth,
Bettina Knoth,
Carola Rentz

TITLE
Die Pflanzen-
Postkarten

TYPE OF WORK
Postcards

CLIENT
Greenpeace Media
GmbH, Hamburg

APPEARED IN
2003

DESIGN
Büro Hamburg JK. PW.
Gesellschaft für Kom-
munikationsdesign
mbH, Hamburg
Bettina Rosenow,
Kerstin Leesch,
Hans Hansen

GINKGO Ginkgo biloba *Fächerblattbäume wachsen seit etwa 190 Millionen Jahren auf der Erde. In China werden die Blätter und deren Extrakte schon lange als Arznei verwendet. Neue Studien zeigen, dass Ginkgo ein wertvolles Mittel gegen eine schlechte Durchblutung des Gehirns ist – und damit verbundene Gedächtnis- und Konzentrationsschwächen.*

www.greenpeace-magazin.de

ecyclingpapier ohne optische Aufheller

TITLE
Blaupause –
Alltagsaufzeichnungen
einer Woche
(junior award)

TYPE OF WORK
Book, undergraduate
dissertation

CLIENT
Fachhochschule Mainz
Prof. Ulysses Voelker
(supervising professor)

DESIGN
Iris Dresler, Mainz

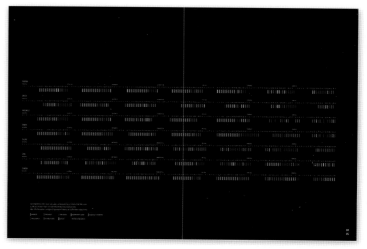

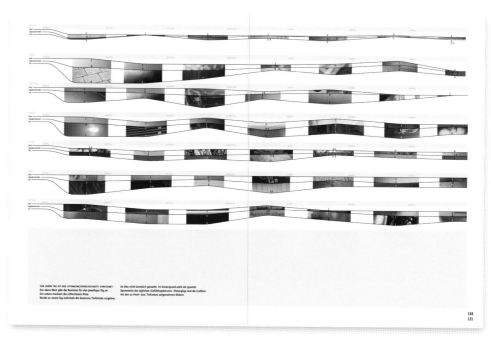

TITLE
PSA 04/05

TYPE OF WORK
Retail kit

CLIENT
Nike Inc, Beaverton

APPEARED IN
02|2004

DESIGN
Nike Inc.
Art direction:
David Young
Graphic design:
Megan Chouinard
Photography:
Phillip Dixon

Two geometric strategies as derived from the analysis of Balla's work form the basic design principles:

1. The motion, rhythm and density of two different bodies moving at the same time generates the form of two major elements.

2. Specific techniques, which activate, spatially articulate and transform the planned programmatic field according to the position and strength of the activating forces.

The internal organisational principle for the two main elements (land mall and air mall) is thus based on crossing, intersecting and overlapping visual connections, thus intertwining both programs and allowing for fluent access between separated areas. Connective points for land and airside are placed on the main traffic nodes around and within the newly planned terminal.

1. Commercial activities of both shorter and longer durations such as shopping, entertainment, wellness, bars, restaurants and services are placed according to the attraction strength of specific zones.

2. Programmatic elements which encourage art purchases host various commercial galleries and are placed into the strips according to the grid of the activated structure itself.

056 Supernova
Sinisa Macedonic

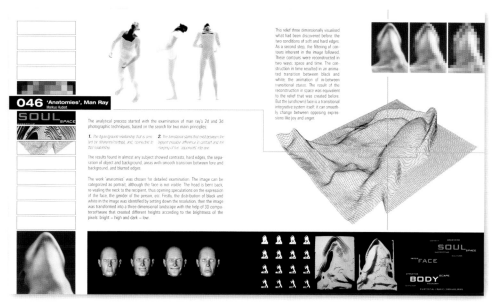

046 'Anatomies', Man Ray
Markus Hudert

The analytical process started with the examination of man ray's 2d and 3d photographic techniques, based on the search for two main principles:

1. The figure/ground relationship that is common for different contrast, and, connected to that relationship.

2. The transitional states that exist between the apparent possible difference in contrast and the merging of two 'documents' into one.

The results found in almost any subject showed contrasts, hard edges, the separation of object and background, areas with smooth transition between fore and background, and blurred edges.

The work 'anatomies' was chosen for detailed examination. The image can be categorized as portrait, although the face is not visible. The head is bent back, re-vealing the neck to the recipient, thus opening speculations on the expression of the face, the gender of the person, etc. Firstly, the distribution of black and white in the image was identified by setting down the resolution, then the image was transformed into a three dimensional landscape with the help of 3D computersoftware that created different heights according to the brightness of the pixels: bright = high and dark = low.

This relief three dimensionally visualised what had been discovered before: the two conditions of soft and hard edges. As a second step, the filtering of contours inherent in the image followed. These contours were reconstructed in two ways: space and time. The construction in time resulted in an animated transition between black and white; the animation of in-between transitional states. The result of the reconstruction in space was equivalent to the relief that was created before. But the (unshown) face is a transitional integrative system itself: it can smoothly change between opposing expressions like joy and anger.

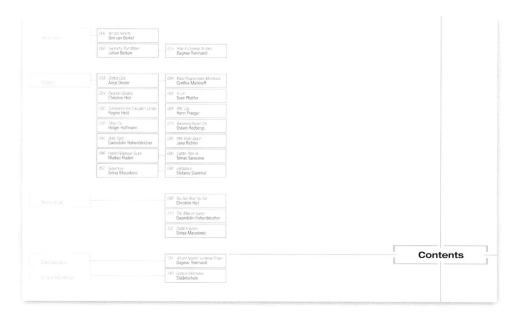

Contents

TITLE
Art and Airports

TYPE OF WORK
Catalogue

CLIENT
Staatliche Hochschule für Bildende Künste Städelschule, Frankfurt/Main

APPEARED IN
12|2003

DESIGN
Sosumi, Frankfurt/Main
Petra Schröder, Dirk von Manteuffel

TITLE
Gaggenau Magazin
2004

TYPE OF WORK
Customer magazine,
catalogue

CLIENT
Gaggenau Haus-
geräte GmbH, Munich

APPEARED IN
05|2004

DESIGN
Gerwin Schmidt
Büro für visuelle
Kommunikation,
Munich
Gerwin Schmidt,
Timo Thurner

TITLE
Boek Beleef 2030

TYPE OF WORK
Book

CLIENT
Essent, Arnhem

APPEARED IN
05|2003

DESIGN
Fabrique [Design,
Communications &
New Media], Delft
Jeroen van Erp,
Pieter Aarts

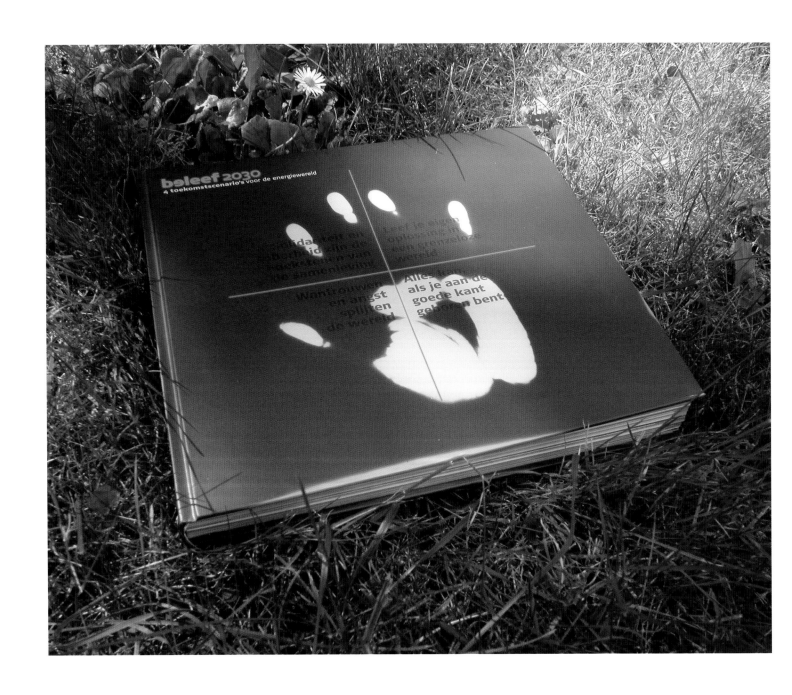

TITLE
Sehen ist lernbar.
Beiträge zur visuellen
Alphabetisierung

TYPE OF WORK
Book, CD-ROM

CLIENT
Europäische
Kommission
Generaldirektion
Bildung und Kultur
Transnational
Cooperation Project
Department, Brussels
Kunstschule Liechten-
stein, Nendeln

APPEARED IN
02|2004

DESIGN
Lürzer Graphik, Götzis
Klaus Lürzer

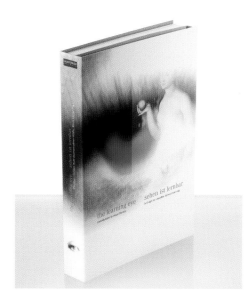

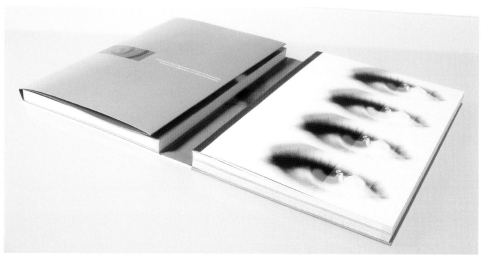

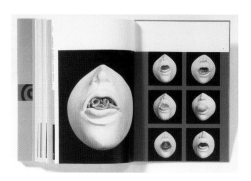

TITLE
Agenda 2003
New York Vertical

TYPE OF WORK
Calendar

CLIENT
Edition Panorama,
Mannheim

DESIGN
Wolff Kommunikation
Carsten Wolff,
Christiane Wolff,
Thomas Rott,
Frankfurt am Main

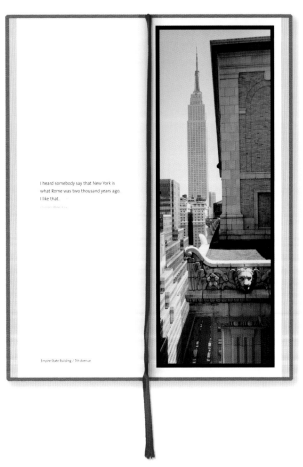

TITLE
Karl Lang
BRIDGES

TYPE OF WORK
Picture book

CLIENT
Edition Panorama,
Mannheim

DESIGN
Wolff Kommunikation
Carsten Wolff,
Christiane Wolff,
Thomas Rott,
Frankfurt am Main

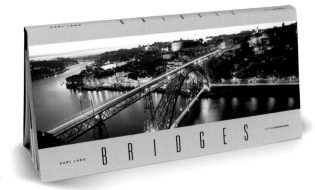

TITLE
Cluster Magazine

TYPE OF WORK
Magazine

CLIENT
Cluster S.R.L., Turin

APPEARED IN
11|2003 – 06|2004

DESIGN
section.d design.com-
munication gmbh,
Vienna
Alois Schwaighofer

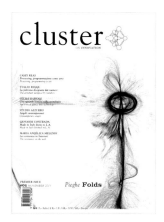

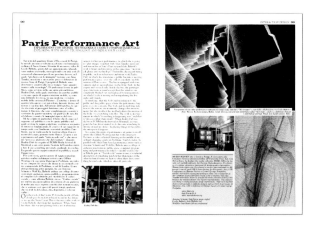

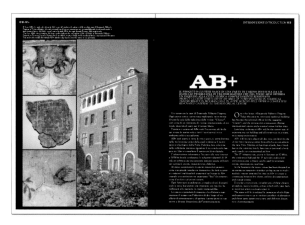

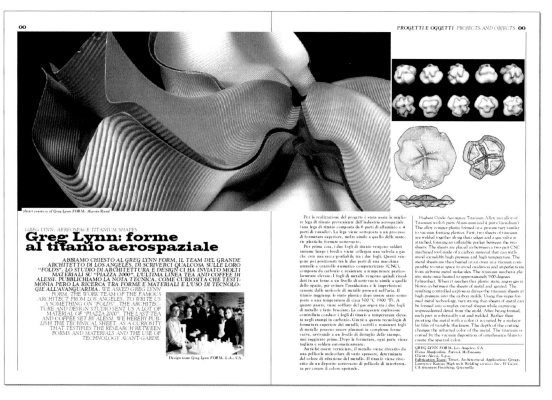

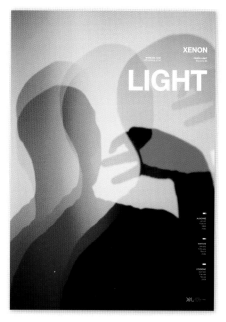

TITLE
LIGHT
Xenon Light magazine

TYPE OF WORK
Magazine

CLIENT
Xenon Light GmbH,
Graz

APPEARED IN
02|2004
06|2004

DESIGN
section.d design.com-
munication gmbh,
Vienna

TITLE
Form meets Function

TYPE OF WORK
Book

CLIENT
AEG Hausgeräte
GmbH, Nuremberg

APPEARED IN
03|2004

DESIGN
Wessel & Daum
Communications,
Meerbusch
Bruno Daum,
Erich Jütten

**Der Mehr-Wert der
Neuen Klasse von AEG.**

Waschen und Trocknen ist mehr als nur notwendiger Aufwand, um saubere Kleidung zu erhalten. Beides steht für die individuelle Pflege unterschiedlichster, empfindlicher Textilien. Auch in der Küche sehen unsere Kunden vieles differenzierter: Kochen ist mehr als rationelles Zubereiten von Speisen. Kühlen ist mehr als sachgerechtes Aufbewahren von Lebensmitteln. Spülen ist mehr als der bequeme Weg zu sauberem Geschirr.

In allen Produktgruppen bietet die Neue Klasse entsprechend mehr Design. Die Formen sind klar und bestimmt, stilvoll und souverän. Hochwertige Materialien wie Edelstahl und Alufer setzen Akzente in jedem Ambiente. Innovative Ausstattungsmerkmale wie die „Longfresh"-0° C-Kalträume oder die komfortable, energiesparende Beladungserkennung mit Dosierempfehlung bei den LAVAMAT Waschautomaten zeigen es. Die Neue Klasse bietet mehr Funktion. Mehr Möglichkeiten. Und mehr Leistung.

Damit ist sie der vorläufige Höhepunkt von nahezu 100 Jahren AEG-Design.

TITLE
Above Zero – Eine
Reise durch Russland

TYPE OF WORK
Book

APPEARED IN
05|2004

DESIGN
Pure Oxygen Design,
Munich
Isabella von Buol,
Franziska Raether,
Alex Lucatello,
Mila Pavan

TITLE
Der BMW 6er

TYPE OF WORK
Book

CLIENT
BMW AG, Munich

APPEARED IN
04|2004

DESIGN
Hoffmann und
Campe Verlag GmbH,
Hamburg
Dirk Linke,
Anna Clea Skoluda,
Sabine Keller,
Armin Ogris,
Gabriele Mayrhofer-
Mik

TITLE
28832 Berlin
Magazin für Druck /
Medien

TYPE OF WORK
Customer magazine

CLIENT
BerlinDruck, Achim

APPEARED IN
04|2002 – 04|2004

DESIGN
Moskito Public
Relations, Bremen
Eckard Christiani,
Tanja Hastedt,
Nicole Waschke

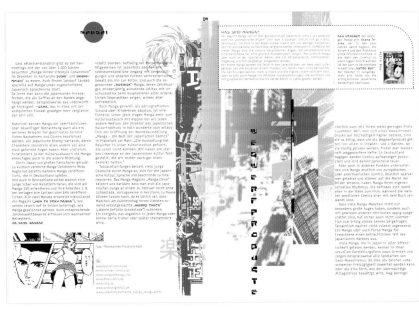

28832 BERLIN
*Magazin für Druck \ Medien * Ausgabe 14*

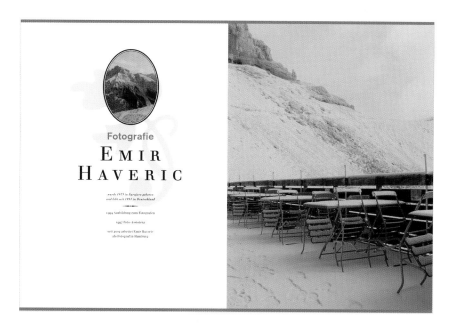

Fotografie
EMIR HAVERIC

WIRTSCHAFT

BEZIEHUNGSKISTEN IN DER KRISE?

BerlinDruck setzt auf Prozessoptimierung

Da mag es noch so viele Wünsche nach antizyklischem Verhalten, nach neuen Märkten, nach Erhöhung des Pro-Kopf-Verbrauches an Papier geben: Drucken ist nun einmal eine Sekundärindustrie, die andere Industrien begleitet. Jede Wirtschaftsrezession bewirkt automatisch eine Krise der Druckindustrie. Das lässt sich aus allen Statistiken der letzten 50 Jahre gut ablesen. Da zudem eine hohe Abhängigkeit von den Werbeausgaben der Industrie zu verzeichnen ist, sieht es zurzeit in der gesamten Druckbranche nicht gut aus. Eine Bestandsaufnahme.

28832 Berlin #17
Magazin für Druck I Medien

TITLE
Helmut Hirler
NATURE 2004

TYPE OF WORK
Calendar

CLIENT
Edition Panorama,
Mannheim

DESIGN
Wolff Kommunikation
Carsten Wolff,
Christiane Wolff,
Thomas Rott,
Frankfurt / Main

helmuthirler|nature0+

ANHANG
Jury | Gestalter | Auftraggeber | Impressum

APPENDIX
Jury | Designers | Clients | Imprint

JURY

Cristina Chiappini studierte Grafikdesign am European Institute of Design in Rom. Seit 1989 ist sie selbstständig und arbeitet sowohl für Privatfirmen als auch für öffentliche Auftraggeber in den Bereichen Publishing, Corporate Design, Webdesign, Interaktive Medien und Motion-Graphic-Television für RAI International. Ihre intensive Lehrtätigkeit begann sie an ihrer ehemaligen Ausbildungsstätte, dem European Istitute of Design. Hier unterrichtete sie Motion Graphics, Typografie und Webdesign und koordinierte den Studiengang Webdesign. Sie hat einen Lehrauftrag an der La Sapienza Universität in Rom im Fachbereich Computertechnologie – IUM Human Computer Interaction. Hier lehrt sie auch „Interactive Space" im Masterstudiengang des Fachbereichs Architektur. Cristina Chiappini ist Mitbegründerin des römischen Media-Lab „334R", das von der öffentlichen Hand finanziert wird. Weiterhin ist sie an verschiedenen interaktiven Forschungsprojekten und Ausstellungen beteiligt. Ihre Website wurde vom ADI Designindex 2003 ausgewählt.

Thomas Kurppa, geboren 1970, erhielt seine Ausbildung von 1996 bis 1999 an der Forsbergs School of Design in Stockholm. 1999 war er als Designer beim Magazin Wallpaper tätig, in den Jahren 2000 bis 2002 war er Art Director bei der Firma Bobby United Design, die er mitbegründet hatte. Seit 2002 ist er Art Director beim Stockholm Design Lab, überdies ist er Dozent an der Forsbergs School of Design. Thomas Kurppa war bereits in Ausstellungen vertreten und gewann mehrere Preise, darunter drei Merit Awards und einen Distinctive Award des Art Directors Club in New York und die Auszeichnung „Young Swedish Design".

Erich Sommer studierte Grafik Design an der Hochschule für Bildende Künste Braunschweig. Nach einem Praktikum bei Anton Stankowski in Stuttgart und einer einjährigen Tätigkeit als Creative Director in einem grafischen Betrieb begann er 1994 bei Total Design. Nach einer Einarbeitungsphase in Amsterdam arbeitete er bis 1999 bei Total Design Maastricht für niederländische und deutsche Auftraggeber im Bereich Corporate Design. Von Ende 1999 bis 2003 war er General Manager von Total Design Köln. Seit 2004 arbeitet er in Köln als selbstständiger Partner der Total Identity Group an Naming- und Corporate-Design-Projekten.

Cristina Chiappini studied graphic design at the European Institute of Design in Rome. She started her own firm in 1989, and has since worked for both private and public companies in the fields of publishing, corporate design, web design, interactive media, and motion-graphic television for RAI International. In parallel she has pursued an intense teaching career starting at her former school, the European Institute of Design. Here she taught motion-graphics, type and web design and also co-ordinated the school's web design course. She is a lecturer at the University of Rome "La Sapienza" in the Department of Computer Technology – IUM Human Computer Interaction and she teaches in the Department of Architecture – "Interactive Space" in the Masters Program. Cristina Chiappini is the co-founder of "334R", Rome's media-lab, which is financed by the local authorities. She continues to participate in various interactive research projects and exhibitions. Her website was selected from the ADI Design Index 2003.

Thomas Kurppa was born in 1970 and received his professional training at the Forsbergs School of Design in Stockholm from 1996 to 1999. In 1999 he was appointed the designer of Wallpaper Magazine before moving on in 2000 to co-found Bobby United Design where he was Art Director until 2002. He has been Art Director of Stockholm Design Lab since 2002, in addition to holding a lectureship at the Forsbergs School of Design. Thomas Kurppa's work has been exhibited at numerous exhibitions and he has won a number of awards including three Merit Awards and a Distinctive Award from the Art Directors Club in New York as well as the "Young Swedish Design" award.

Erich Sommer studied graphic design at the Braunschweig College of Art. Following an internship with Anton Stankowski in Stuttgart and one year as the creative director of a graphic design studio, he began working for Total Design in 1994. After his induction period in Amsterdam, his work involved corporate design for Dutch and German clients of Total Design Maastricht. From the end of 1999 to 2003, he was the general manager of Total Design Cologne. Since 2004 he has worked in Cologne on naming and corporate design projects of the Total Identity Group in his capacity as an independent partner.

JURY

Jean Jacques Schaffner, 1954 in der Schweiz geboren, Grundschulen in Basel. Vorkurs nach dem System Bauhaus an der Kunstgewerbeschule in Basel und Praktikumsaufenthalt als Bildhauer und Besuch der Ecole des Beaux Arts in Paris. Danach Studium an der Fachklasse für Grafik unter Armin Hofmann, Donald Brun, Hermann Eidenbenz, Wolfgang Weingart und Adrian Frutiger. 1977 Gründung des eigenen Ateliers in Basel und Weiterbildung zum TV-Musikregisseur bei Leo Nadelmann sowie Weiterbildung zum Fotografen. Verschiedene Studienaufenthalte in Paris, London/Oxford, San Francisco und an der University of Utah/USA. Seit 1985 Ausbilder für Grafikdesign am Computer und Organisator für Fachseminare zu den Themen Typografie, Packaging Design und Druckvorstufe. Arbeitet zudem als Autor für verschiedene Fachzeitschriften zu den Themen Design, interaktive Kommunikation und Packaging Design. Sein Unternehmen, die Schaffner & Conzelmann Designersfactory mit Sitz in Basel/Schweiz ist eine Full-Service-Agentur und umfasst sämtliche Dienstleistungen der visuellen Kommunikation. Von 2000 bis 2003 war er Präsident der Pan European Brand and Packaging Design Association PDA und hielt bei vielen Kongressen rund um den Globus Vorträge und Vorlesungen. Er ist ebenfalls in vielen Design-Jurys aktiv. Arbeitet heute mit seinem Team sowohl als Fotograf wie auch als Designer.

Frido Steinen-Broo, geboren 1952, Schriftsetzerlehre, Studium in Berlin, Bordeaux und Lausanne, Abschluss an der Hochschule der Künste in Berlin. Danach zweieinhalb Jahre Tätigkeit im Friedrich Verlag, anschließend freiberuflich tätig in Berlin. Von 1993 bis 1996 als Seniordesigner bei Metadesign, u.a. Entwicklung der Erscheinungsbilder für den Springer-Verlag, Heidelberg und Mabeg, Soest. Seit März 1996 wohnhaft in Spanien und 1997 Gründung von eStudio Calamar mit den Schwerpunkten Corporate- und Editorialdesign.

Stefan Ytterborn, Jahrgang 1963, ist Präsident der Firma Ytterborn & Fuentes, die er 1996 gründete. Zusammenarbeit mit vielen renommierten Unternehmen wie iittala, Ericsson, Saab und Boston Consulting Group, dabei Entwicklung von Corporate Identities, Strategieberatung und Produktentwicklung. Daneben ist Stefan Ytterborn als Dozent und Ausstellungskurator aktiv, ist Mitglied verschiedener Jurys und Ausschüsse wie z.B. dem European Design Prize 1996, dem Elle Interior Scholarship, der Swedish Association of Advertising und der Swedish Industrial Design Foundation. Zu seinen zahlreichen Auszeichnungen gehören der Good Design Award, Japan, iF Design Award, Marie Claire Award, Guldägget und The Golden Key of Finnish Craftsmanship.

Jean Jacques Schaffner, born in 1954 in Zurich, Switzerland, attended elementary school in Basle. Thereafter he participated in a preliminary course in the Bauhaus method at the Technical Art College in Basle and did his apprenticeship as a sculptor with lessons at the Ecole des Beaux Arts in Paris. He attended master graphics classes taught by Armin Hofmann, Donald Brun, Hermann Eidenbenz, Adrian Frutinger and others. In 1977 he founded his own design studio in Basle but also qualified as a photographer and, under the tutelage of Leo Nadelmann, as a music film director. Never being able to quench his curiosity, he attended various university courses in Paris, London/Oxford, San Francisco and at the University of Utah. Since 1985 he has taught computer-based graphic design, organized seminars on design and pre-print, and written articles on the topics of design, interactive communication and packaging design for a number of trade journals. His company Schaffner & Conzelmann, Designersfactory, located in Basle, is a full service agency in the field of visual communication. From 2000 to 2003 he was President of the Pan European Brand and Packaging Design Association PDA giving lectures and holding presentations at numerous congresses around the globe. He is also an active participant in a number of design juries. Currently he devotes his time to his team, working both as a designer and as a photographer.

Frido Steinen-Broo, born 1952, apprenticeship as a type-setter, studied in Berlin, Bordeaux and Lausanne, graduated at the Hochschule der Künste in Berlin. Following this, two and a half years work at Friedrich Verlag (publishers), and then freelance work in Berlin. From 1993 to 1996 senior designer for Metadesign, with work including the development of the corporate image of Springer, a publishing house, Heidelberg and Mabeg, Soest. He has been living in Spain since March 1996 and founded eStudio Calamar in 1997, which focuses on corporate and editorial design.

Stefan Ytterborn, born in 1963, is President of Ytterborn & Fuentes, which he founded in 1996. His clients include iittala, Ericsson, Saab and Boston Consulting Group, for whom he has worked on projects ranging from corporate identity to advising on strategy and product development. In addition, Stefan Ytterborn is an active lecturer and exhibition curator. He is a member of a number of juries and committees, including the 1996 European Design Prize, the Elle Interior Scholarship, the Swedish Association of Advertising and the Swedish Industrial Design Foundation. To name just a few of his numerous awards and distinctions: the Good Design Award, Japan, iF Design Award, Marie Claire Award, Guldägget and The Golden Key of Finnish Craftsmanship.

JURY

Mervyn Kurlansky wurde 1936 in Johannesburg/Südafrika geboren. Er besuchte die Central School of Art and Design in London und war anschließend drei Jahre selbstständig. Danach arbeitete er fünf Jahre lang als Graphics Director bei Planning Unit, den Designberatern von Knoll International, 1969 kam er zu Crosby/Fletcher/Forbes. Bis 1993 war er bei Pentagram (1972 von ihm mitbegründet), seit 1993 lebt und arbeitet er in Dänemark. Er erhielt u.a. den Gold Award des Package Design Council, Silver Awards der Designers and Art Directors Association und einen Silver Award des New Yorker Art Directors Club. Er hat zahlreiche Lehraufträge und ist Mitglied mehrerer Designgremien. Er ist Präsident von Icograda (International Council of Graphic Design Associations), Fellow der Chartered Society of Designers, der International Society of Typographic Designers und der Royal Society for the Encouragement of Art Manufactures & Commerce. Er ist Mitglied der Alliance Graphique Internationale und des dänischen Designerverbandes.

Guy Schockaert wurde 1949 in Courtrai geboren. Nach seiner Ausbildung am Institut Saint-Luc in Brüssel war er Assistent bei Michel Olyff, bis er sich schließlich 1971 als Grafikdesigner selbstständig machte. Noch heute führt er sein Büro Ad hoc Design, in dem er Markenerscheinungen, Broschüren und Bücher für zahlreiche Auftraggeber wie Alfac, 3M, Plantin, Sic oder RTBF realisiert. Mit seiner Professionalität, seiner Leidenschaft für Typografie und seinem Interesse an neuen Techniken steht Schockaert mit seiner Arbeit für „Strenge und Gefühl" im Dienste der Botschaft. Er hält außerdem Vorträge, ist in der Lehre tätig und engagiert sich unermüdlich in Berufsorganisationen wie dem Conseil International des Associations de Design Graphique (Icograda), dessen Präsident er 1997 bis 1999 war. Guy Schockaert gehört zu den Initiatoren von „Design for the World", einer Organisation, die „Design"-Lösungen für humanitäre Probleme sucht. Seit 2003 ist er Präsident der Ydesign Foundation.

Kurt Weidemann absolvierte nach einem Jahrzehnt Kriegsgefangenschaft eine Schriftsetzerlehre in Lübeck, studierte an der Staatlichen Akademie der Bildenden Künste in Stuttgart und arbeitete als Schriftleiter beim „Druckspiegel". Heute arbeitet der Designer, Typograf und Texter nach umfangreichen Lehrtätigkeiten (Stuttgart, Karlsruhe, Koblenz) als Berater und Gutachter großer Unternehmen. So konzipierte er für den Daimler-Benz-Konzern das Erscheinungsbild. Auch die Erscheinungsbilder der Firmen Coop, Merck und Zeiss sowie das der Deutschen Bahn AG wurden von ihm entwickelt. 1995 wurde er mit dem Lucky Strike Designer Award, Europas höchstdotiertem Designer-Preis, und dem Verdienstorden 1. Klasse der Bundesrepublik geehrt.

Mervyn Kurlansky was born in Johannesburg, South Africa in 1936. He trained at the Central School of Art and Design in London and then spent three years in freelance practice. This was followed by five years as graphics director of Planning Unit, the design consultancy service of Knoll International. In 1969 he joined Crosby/Fletcher/Forbes and in 1972 co-founded Pentagram, from which he resigned in 1993 to live and work in Denmark. He has won a number of important awards, including a gold award from the Package Designers Council, silver awards from the Designers and Art Directors Association and a silver award from the New York Art Directors Club. He lectures extensively and has served on numerous panels judging design. He is President of Icograda (the International Council of Graphic Design Associations), a Fellow of the Chartered Society of Designers, the International Society of Typographic Designers and the Royal Society for the Encouragement of Arts, Manufactures & Commerce. He is a member of Alliance Graphique Internationale and the Association of Danish Designers.

Guy Schockaert was born in Courtrai, Belgium in 1949. After studying graphic arts and visual communication at the Institut Saint-Luc, Bruxelles he became an assistant to Michel Olyff before becoming self-employed as a graphic designer in 1971. His graphic studio "Ad hoc Design" specializes in corporate identity, books and brochures for a range of clients including Alfac, 3M, Plantin, Sic and RTBF. Schockaert advocates "rigour and emotion" in the message. He has given numerous talks, has been active in teaching since the beginning of his career and is a tireless proponent of professional organizations such as Icograda (International Council of Graphic Design Associations) where he was President from 1997 to 1999. He is one of the initiators of "Design for the World", an organisation that is dedicated to finding "design" solutions to humanitarian problems. Since 2003 he has been President of Ydesign Foundation.

Kurt Weidemann spent one year as a prisoner of war before serving as an apprentice typesetter in Lübeck prior to studying at the State Academy of Arts in Stuttgart. He then became editor of "Der Druckspiegel". Aside from his extensive teaching work (Stuttgart, Karlsruhe, Koblenz), the designer, typographer and copywriter works as a consultant for large enterprises, creating the corporate design and design guidelines for Daimler-Benz, for example. He also developed the corporate identity of Coop, Merck and Zeiss as well as Deutsche Bahn AG. In 1995 he was honoured with the Lucky Strike Designer Award, the most highly regarded design award in Europe and with the Order of Merit (First Class) of the Federal Republic of Germany.

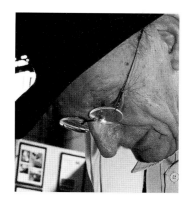

aexea Integrierte
Kommunikation
Saim Alkan
Firnhaberstraße 5
D-70174 Stuttgart
www.aexea.de
186

Alessandri GmbH
Rufgasse 3
Fabrik im Hof
A-1090 Wien
www.alessandri-design.at
218

Anna B. Design
Erkelenzdamm 11-13
D-10999 Berlin
www.annabdesign.de
276

ART+COM AG
Kleiststraße 23-26
D-10787 Berlin
86

Art+Work= Werbeagentur
Berner Straße 38
D-60437 Frankfurt/Main
www.artundwork.com
171

Artefakt Industriekultur
Liebigstraße 50-52
D-64293 Darmstadt
www.artefakt.de
217

ASATSU-DK INC
13-1, Tsukiji 1-chome
Chuo-ku
J-Tokyo 104-8172
www.adk.jp
76

Atelier Markgraph GmbH
Hamburger Allee 45
D-60486 Frankfurt/Main
www.markgraph.de
236

bangertprojects
Dr. Albrecht Bangert
Blütenweg 10
D-79650 Schopfheim
www.bangertverlag.com
232

Barbara + Gerd Baumann
Taubentalstraße 4/1
D-73525 Schwäbisch Gmünd
www.baumannandbaumann.com
75

BBDO Campaign GmbH
Königsallee 92
D-40212 Düsseldorf
www.bbdo.de
146

BBDO InterOne GmbH
Schulterblatt 58
D-20357 Hamburg
www.bbdo-interone.de
99, 100, 101

Beaufort 8 GmbH
Kernerstraße 50
D-70182 Stuttgart
www.beaufort8.de
190

Daniel Becker
Schönhauser Allee 39a
D-10435 Berlin
www.goldenerwesten.net
www.fh-potsdam.de
106

Beierarbeit
Sattelmeyerweg 1
D-33609 Bielefeld
www.beierarbeit.de
191

Angélique Bolter
Owingerstraße 23
D-88662 Überlingen
64

BRANDIT
Marketing und Kommunikation
Mittelstraße 12-14
D-50672 Köln
www.brandit.de
46, 279

Erich Brechbühl [Mixer]
Löwenplatz 5
CH-6004 Luzern
www.mixer.ch
254

Wolfgang Breuninger
Kommunikationsdesign
Friedrichstraße 11a
D-71686 Remseck am Neckar
www.kommunikationsdesign.de
289

Bruce B. GmbH
Rosenbergstraße 50/1
D-70176 Stuttgart
www.bruce-b.com
134, 304

Prof. Hartmut Brückner
Büro Brückner + Partner
Plantage 13
D-28215 Bremen
www.buero-brueckner.de
284

Bruketa & Zinic
Zavrtnica 17
HR-10000 Zagreb
www.bruketa-zinic.com
207, 219

Melanie Brunner
Tägermoosstraße 5
CH-8280 Kreuzlingen
www.formidable.ch
216

Martin Buecker
Schlosserstraße 15
D-70180 Stuttgart
239

Buero 16
Lorenz-Mandl-Gasse 33
A-1160 Wien
www.buero16.com
197

burbulla.design
Graefestraße 1
D-10967 Berlin
www.burbulla.com
306

büro diffus GmbH
Mozartstraße 51
D-70180 Stuttgart
www.diffus.com
185, 283, 286

Büro Hamburg JK. PW.
Gesellschaft für
Kommunikationsdesign mbH
Hohe Brücke 1
D-20459 Hamburg
www.buero-hamburg.de
318

Büro4
Gestaltung und Kommunikation
Bäckerstraße 52
CH-8004 Zürich
www.buero4.ch
72, 170

Ca Concepts
Christian Aichner
Am Südfeld 2
D-86937 Scheuring
www.ca-concepts.de
142

Jana Cerno Design
Comeniusstraße 8
D-81667 München
142

CID Lab.
2-4-3-603 Uchihommachi
Chuo-ku
J-Osaka 540-0026
www.cid-lab.info
132

Corporate Marketing
Sohnckestraße 12
D-81479 München
www.cmarketing.de
66

de-construct
10-18 Vestry Street
GB-London N1 73E
www.de-construct.com
105

Design 3
Jolanda Luethy
Bruggerstraße 37
CH-5400 Baden
177

Design: MW
149 Wooster St.
USA-New York, NY 10012
www.designmw.com
290

Designliga
Waltherstraße 7a
D-80337 München
www.designliga.de
123

Die Firma GmbH
Schwalbacher Straße 74
D-65183 Wiesbaden
www.diefirma.de
94, 95

Iris Dresler
Thomas-Mann-Straße 5a
D-55122 Mainz
319

Agentur E
Schlesische Straße 26/D
D-10997 Berlin
www.contact-e.com
144

Redaktion Echtzeit 02
c/o Fachhochschule Potsdam
Fachbereich Design
Pappelallee 8-9
D-14469 Berlin
www.echtzeit02.de
312

Eggers + Diaper
Heckmannufer 6a
D-10997 Berlin
www.eggers-diaper.com
258

engenhart visuelle kommunikation
unit von lichtpunkt//netzwerk
Postfach 02 31
D-71350 Winnenden
www.engenhart.com
165

Epigram
75 Sophia Road
Singapore 228156
www.epigram.com.sg
204

Fabrique [Design, Communications
& New Media]
Oude Delft 201
NL-2611 HD Delft
www.fabrique.nl
324

Fachhochschule Düsseldorf
Georg-Glock-Straße 15
D-40474 Düsseldorf
www.fh-duesseldorf.de
317

Fachhochschule Wiesbaden
Unter den Eichen 5
D-65195 Wiesbaden
www.fh-wiesbaden.de
297

Factor Design AG
Schulterblatt 58
D-20357 Hamburg
www.factordesign.com
80, 172, 173, 174

Hoffmann und Campe Verlag
GmbH
Harvestehuder Weg 42
D-20149 Hamburg
www.hoca.de
333

Daniela Höhmann
Schleswiger Straße 61
D-42107 Wuppertal
www.hoehmann-design.de
141

Felix Hornung
Severinstraße 1
D-50678 Köln
140

Alexandra Höver
Gladbacher Straße 43
D-40219 Düsseldorf
www.vk-hoever.de
307

Hideki Inaba Design
PK108/B1 2-32-13 Matsubara
Setagaya-ku
J-Tokyo 156-0043
www.hidekiinaba.com
78, 316

Incorporate
Münzstraße 13
D-10178 Berlin
www.incorporate.de
198

Peyote cross design concepts
Irschitz GmbH & Co KEG
Grünentorgasse 19/22
A-1090 Wien
www.irschitz.com
www.peyote.cc
235

Jäger & Jäger
Heiligenbreite 52
D-88662 Überlingen
www.jaegerundjaeger.de
26

Siena Jakobi
Manteuffelstraße 2
D-28203 Bremen
www.gfg-bremen.de
301

Daniel Janssen
Saarlandstraße 13
D-22303 Hamburg
www.bfgjanssen.de
32

Stephanie + Ralf de Jong
Typografie
Schlossteichstraße 3
D-34131 Kassel
www.ralfdejong.de
268

Jung von Matt
Glashüttenstraße 38
D-20357 Hamburg
www.jvm.de
217

Jung von Matt/Elbe GmbH
Glashüttenstraße 38
D-20357 Hamburg
www.jvm.de
107

Emanuela Karantinaki
Bismarckstraße110
D-28203 Bremen
311

Eric Kessels
At Kesselskramer
Lauriergracht 39
NL-1001 EA Amsterdam
www.kesselskramer.nl
175

kleiner und bold GmbH
Neue Schönhauser Straße 19
D-10178 Berlin
www.kleinerundbold.com
97

KMS Team GmbH
Deroystraße 3-5
D-80335 München
www.kms-team.de
42, 163, 164, 166, 184, 240

Moritz Koepp
Eberswalder Straße 22
D-10437 Berlin
www.goldenerwesten.net
106

kognito gestaltung
Alt-Moabit 62-63
D-10555 Berlin
www.kognito.de
282

Designgruppe Koop
Obere Wank 12
D-87484 Nesselwang
www.designgruppe-koop.de
153

KP&Z Werbeagentur GmbH
Berkstraße 11
D-48163 Münster
www.kp-z.de
131

Kreutz & Partner Kommunikation
Humboldtstraße 18
D-40237 Düsseldorf
www.kreutzundpartner.de
277

Atelier Bernd Kuchenbeiser
Theresienstraße 56 Hof 1
D-80333 München
www.kuchenbeiser.de
112

Martina Kurz
Gaußstraße 75
D-70193 Stuttgart
70

Eva Schubert
Kirchbergstraße 24
D-64625 Bensheim
227

section.d design.communication
gmbh
Praterstraße 66
A-1020 Wien
www.sectiond.at
328, 329

Segura Inc
1110 N. Milwaukee Ave.
USA-Chicago, IL 60622-4017
www.segura-inc.com
22

Yvonne Seidel
Wilhelm-Raabe-Straße 5
D-70199 Stuttgart
186

serres, design.
Schleusenstraße 8
D-45525 Hattingen
www.serres-design.de
252

Shigeno Araki Design Office
2-4-18, Bandai
Sumiyoshi-ku
J-Osaka 558-0055
220

Sign Kommunikation GmbH
Oskar-von-Miller-Straße 14
D-60314 Frankfurt/Main
www.sign.de
45

Eva Simonsen
Kirchbergstraße 24
D-64625 Bensheim
227

Smakdesign GbR
Grabenstraße 149a
D-47057 Duisburg
www.smakdesign.de
257

S/O Project
Chungdam-dong 36-1
Kangnam-gu
ROK-Seoul 135100
www.soproject.com
199

Solar Initiative
's Gravenhekje 1 A
NL-1011 TG Amsterdam
www.solarinitiative.com
www.solarphotography.com
183, 263

Sosumi
Kommunikationsgestaltung
Cassellastraße 30-32
D-60386 Frankfurt/Main
www.sosumi.net
321

Springer & Jacoby Design
Poststraße 37-39
D-20354 Hamburg
www.sj.com
314

Ulf Constantin Stein
Schillerstraße 15
D-44147 Dortmund
www.ulfstein.de
315

Andreas Stiller
Weißenburgstraße 15
D-42107 Wuppertal
www.andreasstiller.de
253

strichpunkt
Schönleinstraße 8a
D-70184 Stuttgart
www.strichpunkt-design.de
58, 214

Studio für Fotografie
Markus Steur
Postkutschenstraße 14a
D-44287 Dortmund
www.steur.de
256

Studio International
Boris Ljubičić
Buconjiceva 43/2
HR-10000 Zagreb
www.studio-international.com
264

Sandra Tebbe
Staderstraße 114
D-28205 Bremen
311

Tillmanns, Ogilvy & Mather
GmbH & Co. KG
Am Handelshafen 2-4
D-40221 Düsseldorf
www.ogilvy.com
200

TOCA ME GmbH
Böhmerwaldstraße 57
D-85737 Ismaning
www.toca-me.com
104

Total Identity BV
Paalbergweg 42
NL-1105 BV Amsterdam
P.O. Box 12480
NL-1100 AL Amsterdam
www.totalidentity.nl
178

Niklaus Troxler Design
Postfach
CH-6130 Willisau
www.troxlerart.ch
52, 269

büro uebele
visuelle kommunikation
Heusteigstraße 94a
D-70180 Stuttgart
www.uebele.com
156, 158, 230, 292

UNA (Amsterdam) designers
Korte Papaverweg 7 A
NL-1032 KA Amsterdam
www.unadesigners.nl
187, 280, 281

Universal Corporate
Communications, Inc.
#701, Asem Tower
159-1, Samsung-dong
Kangnam-gu
ROK-Seoul 135798
www.ucc.co.kr
205, 206

Visualis GmbH
Friedensstraße 87
D-75173 Pforzheim
www.visualis.de
222

Judith Wagner
Lichtstraße 29
D-40235 Düsseldorf
www.judithwagner.de
296

Waidmann/Post
Kaffeetwete 3
D-38100 Braunschweig
www.waidmannpost.de
61

weissraum.de(sign)
Wohlers Allee 24a
D-22767 Hamburg
www.weissraum.de
122, 210

Werbewelt Interactive GmbH
Rheinlandstraße 10
D-71636 Ludwigsburg
www.werbewelt.com
91

Wessel & Daum Communications
Am Meerkamp 26
D-40667 Meerbusch
www.wessel-daum.de
330

Carsten M. Wolff /
Christina Wolff / Thomas Rott
Laubestraße 22
D-60594 Frankfurt/Main
www.wolff-kommunikation.de
326, 327, 336

Matthias Wörle
Donaustraße 50
D-28199 Bremen
311

wppt:kommunikation GmbH
Treppenstraße 17-19
D-42115 Wuppertal
www.wppt.de
308

yama inc. – Büro für Gestaltung
Ingo Ditges
Alexanderstraße 164b
D-70180 Stuttgart
www.yama.de
186

Alexandra Zemp
Frauenfelderstraße 5
CH-8570 Weinfelden
www.designcode.ch
216

Accell
Unter den Buchen 6
D-38700 Braunlage
45

Acht Frankfurt digital solutions
Hanauer Landstraße 11–13
D-60314 Frankfurt/Main
116

adidas-Salomon AG
World of Sports
D-91074 Herzogenaurach
www.adidas.de
194

AEG Hausgeräte GmbH
Muggenhofer Straße 135
D-90429 Nürnberg
330

AKF Bank
Friedrichstraße 51
D-42105 Wuppertal
www.akf.de
193

AML Licht + Design
Wiener Platz 7 RGB
D-81667 München
www.axelmeiselicht.de
155

Ando bv
Mercuriusweg 37
NL-2516 AW Den Haag
www.ando.net
278

Bacardi España SA
c/ Fernando Bacardi, 14
E-08100 Mollet del Valles
(Barcelona)
211

Base Detall Sport SA
c/ Sancho de Avila, 83
E-08018 Barcelona
48

BDA Bund Deutscher Architekten
Zellerstraße 82
D-70180 Stuttgart
www.bda-architekten.de
286

Beams Co., Ltd.
7F, 3-21-5 Tingumae
Shibuya-ku
J-Tokyo 150-0001
316

Belux AG
Bremgarterstraße 109
CH-5610 Wohlen
www.belux.com
177

Bergische Universität Wuppertal
Haspeler Straße 27
D-42285 Wuppertal
37, 141

Berlin Biennale
Auguststraße 69
D-10117 Berlin
260

BerlinDruck
Oskar-Schulze-Straße 12
D-28832 Achim
www.berlindruck.de
334

BISS e.V.
Königinstraße 77
D-80539 München
139

BMG Ariola Classics GmbH
Neumarkter Straße 28
D-81673 München
94

BMW AG
Petuelring 130
D-80788 München
www.bmw.com
99, 100, 333

BMW AG
Brand Communication MINI
Petuelring 130
D-80788 München
www.mini.com
101

Irma Boom Office
Kerkstraat 104
NL-1017 GP Amsterdam
www.irmaboom.nl
34

Bosch Transferzentrum
Venture Capital
Ingersheimer Straße 16
D-70499 Stuttgart
190

Botanisches Museum Berlin-Dahlem
Königin-Luise-Straße 6-8
D-14191 Berlin
106

British Library
96 Euston Road
GB-London NW1 2DB
258

Michael Broger Weinbau
Schnellberg 1
CH-8561 Ottoberg
www.broger-weinbau.ch
216

atelierbrückner
Quellenstraße 7
D-70376 Stuttgart
283

Bundesministerium der Finanzen
Wilhelmstraße 97
D-10117 Berlin
www.bundesfinanzministerium.de
246, 247

Bundesministerium für
wirtschaftliche Zusammenarbeit
und Entwicklung
Friedrich-Ebert-Allee 40
D-53113 Bonn
www.bmz.de
253

Carpet Concept
Objekt-Teppichboden GmbH
Bunzlauer Straße 7
D-33719 Bielefeld
www.carpet-concept.de
96

Centrum Beeldende Kunst (CBK)
Dordrecht
Voorstraat 180
NL-3311 ES Dordrecht
www.cbkdordrecht.nl
263

Chubu Electric Power Co., Inc.
1 Toshin-cho
Higashi-ku
J-Nagoya 461-8680
132

SintLucas (School for
Communication and Design)
Grote Beemd 24
P.O. Box 120
NL-5280 AC Boxtel
www.sintlucas.nl
175

SK Telecom
IR Office SK Telecom
99 Seorin-dong
Jongro-gu
ROK-Seoul 110728
www.sktelecom.com
206

Martita Slewe
Slewe Gallery
Kerkstraat 105 A
NL-1017 GD Amsterdam
www.slewe.nl
34

smart gmbh
Leibnizstraße 2
D-71032 Böblingen
www.smart.com
304

Sportswear Company
Via Confine 2161
I-41017 Ravarino
144

Staatliche Hochschule für
Bildende Künste
Städelschule
Dürerstraße 10
D-60596 Frankfurt/Main
www.staedelschule.de
321

Staatliche Museen Kassel
Schloss Wilhelmshöhe
D-34131 Kassel
268

Staatl. Vermögens- und
Hochbauamt Pforzheim
Simmlerstraße 9
D-75172 Pforzheim
230

Stiftung Buchkunst,
Frankfurt und Leipzig
Adickesallee 1
D-60322 Frankfurt/Main
311

Stiftung Saarländischer Kulturbesitz
Bismarckstraße 11-19
D-66111 Saarbrücken
166

Studio für Fotografie
Markus Steur
Postkutschenstraße 14a
D-44287 Dortmund
www.steur.de
256

Süddeutsche Zeitung GmbH
Sendlinger Straße 8
D-80331 München
145

TDR
Obala V. Nazora 1
HR-52210 Rovinj
219

Tenuta Kornell-Staves
I-39018 Siebeneich (Bozen)
161

TOCA ME GmbH
Böhmerwaldstraße 57
D-85737 Ismaning
www.toca-me.com
104

Transsolar Energietechnik
Curiestraße 2
D-70563 Stuttgart
158

Type Directors Club
127 West 25th St.
USA-New York, NY 10001
www.tdc.org
290, 292

UNA (Amsterdam) designers
Korte Papaverweg 7 A
NL-1032 KA Amsterdam
www.unadesigners.nl
280, 281

Universal Music GmbH
Stralauer Allee 1
D-10245 Berlin
44

Unsere kleinen Brüder
und Schwestern
Ritterstraße 9
D-76137 Karlsruhe
126

VdW Verband deutscher
Werbefilmproduzenten e.V.
Poststraße 33/VI
D-20354 Hamburg
www.werbefilmproduzenten.de
www.vdw-award.de
118, 167

Verlag Hermann Schmidt Mainz
Robert-Koch-Straße 8
D-55129 Mainz
214

Verlag Hermann Schmidt Mainz /
TDC Deutschland
Robert-Koch-Straße 8
D-55129 Mainz
292

Volvo Car Germany GmbH
Ringstraße 38-44
D-50996 Köln
www.volvocars.com
102

Whirlpool Europe Srl
Viale Borghi 27
I-21025 Comerio (VA)
www.whirlpool.com
310

Bankhaus Wölbern
Herrengraben 74
D-20459 Hamburg
198

Würth Medien GmbH
Jahnstraße 15
D-73635 Rudersberg
www.wuerthmedien.de
186

Xenon Light GmbH
Auer-Welsbach-Gasse 36
A-8055 Graz
329

Zisterzienserstift Zwettl
A-3910 Zwettl
26

IMPRESSUM|IMPRINT

Herausgeber | Editor	Peter Zec
Projektleitung | Project management	Elmar Schüller, Sabine Wöll
Projektorganisation | Project organisation	Sabine Meier, Marzena Stochniol, Kurt C. Reinhardt
Übersetzung | Translation	Bruce Stout
Redaktion | Editorial	Petra Kiedaisch, Anja Schrade
Gestaltung | Design	Christof Gassner, Darmstadt
Layout	Gabi Koch
Jurorenfotos | Jury Photos	Fotografie Peter Wieler, Essen
Produktion | Production	avcommunication Gunther Heeb
Lithographie | Lithography	ctrl-s prepress GmbH
Druck | Printing	Leibfarth+Schwarz GmbH+Co. KG Dettingen|Erms
Papier | Paper	150g/m², Dullcoat
© Copyright	2004/2005 avedition GmbH, Ludwigsburg

Alle Rechte vorbehalten | All rights reserved

ISBN 3-89986-033-0
Printed in Germany

Der Grand Prix wird gesponsert von Krenzler Graf Biermann OHG, Allianz Group, Essen. Der Junior Prize wird gesponsert von der AGD Alliance of German Designers.

The Grand Prix is sponsored by Krenzler Graf Biermann OHG, Allianz Group, Essen. The Junior Prize is sponsored by the AGD Alliance of German Designers.

Allianz
Krenzler Graf Biermann OHG

AGD

In Kooperation mit |
In cooperation with:
AGD Alliance of German Designers; www.agd.de
AGI Alliance Graphique Internationale; www.a-g-i.org
BNO Beroepsorganisatie Nederlandse Ontwerpers; www.bno.nl
Deutsches Plakatmuseum, Essen
KIDP Korea Institute of Design Promotion; www.designdb.com
SGD Swiss Graphic Designers; www.sgd.ch
www.100-beste-plakate.de